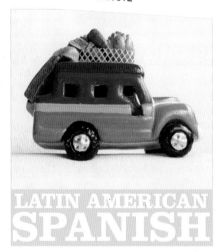

LATIN AMERICAN
SPANISH

With menu decoder, survival guide and two-way dictionary

Thomas Cook
Thomas Cook **Publishing**

www.thomascookpublishing.com

Survival guide..................49

Emergencies.....................59

Dictionary.......................63

Quick reference...............95

How to use this guide

The ten chapters in this guide are colour-coded to help you find what you're looking for. These colours are used on the tabs of the pages and in the contents on the opposite page and above.

For quick reference, you'll find some basic expressions on the inside front cover and essential emergency phrases on the inside back cover. There is also a handy reference section for numbers, measurements, days, times and months at the back of the guide.

Front cover @ Thomas Cook Publishing
Cover design/artwork by Sharon Edwards
Photo credits: Sue Crocker (p17) and László Harri Németh (p63)

Produced by The Content Works Ltd
www.thecontentworks.com
Design concept: Mike Wade
Layout: Tika Stefano
Text: Cristina Hernández & Hiram Espina
Editing: Begoña Juarros & Amanda Castleman
Proofing: Wendy Janes
Project editor: Begoña Juarros
Management: Lisa Plumridge & Rik Mulder

Published by Thomas Cook Publishing
A division of Thomas Cook Tour Operations Limited
Company Registration No 1450464 England
PO Box 227, Unit 18, Coningsby Road
Peterborough PE3 8SB, United Kingdom
email: books@thomascook.com
www.thomascookpublishing.com
+ 44 (0) 1733 416477

ISBN-13: 978-1-84157-720-3

First edition © 2007 Thomas Cook Publishing
Text © 2007 Thomas Cook Publishing

Project editor: Kelly Pipes
Production/DTP: Steven Collins

Printed and bound in Italy by Printer Trento

Introduction

From the Mayan and Aztec pyramids in Central America to the palm-fringed beaches and turquoise waters of the Caribbean; from the rich flora and fauna of the Central American rainforests to the snow-covered Andes and Machu Picchu, symbol of the Inca empire; Latin America is a huge, fascinating and extreme region. You can travel thousands of miles, from Tijuana on the US-Mexican border, down to Patagonia in the continent's south, and always make yourself understood in the same language. Spanish is also the world's fourth most common language, after Chinese, Hindi and English, and 400 million people call it their mother tongue. So, what are you waiting for? ¡Hable español!

Introduction

5

Introduction

Spanish is descended from Latin, like French and Italian. 700 years of Moorish influence on the Iberian peninsula have also left their traces. Words like **alfombra** (carpet) and **almohada** (pillow) reflect these Arabic roots.

More than 500 years have passed since Columbus set sail and – as a result – introduced the Spanish language on the American continent, where it took a distinct development from the "motherland". The local, indigenous peoples, Africans brought to America as slaves and streams of immigration from Europe all had their influences on the way Spanish evolved in the various countries of the "New World".

Argentinian and Uruguayan Spanish have a particularity worth mentioning: instead of **tú** ("you" for one person) the word **vos** is generally used. Apart from that, all countries have their own idioms and a list of words merely used locally. The various words used for bus in colloquial language are a good example. But if you ask for the **autobús** you'll be understood everywhere.

False friends

English and Spanish have quite a few similar terms. Sometimes it's even possible to guess a term by adding "o" or "a".

Occasionally that tactic goes horribly, horribly wrong. Here are some "false friends": words that resemble each other, but express very different ideas:

Embarazada – pregnant (not embarrassed)

Sensible – sensitive (not sensible)

Constipada – to have a cold (not to be constipated)

Simpático – friendly (not sympathetic)

Petróleo – oil (not petrol)

Librería – bookshop (not a library)

6

Grammar

Spanish is a very phonetic language: You say what you see – a real boon for beginners.

Nouns fall into three groups: masculine (**el vino**), feminine (**la cerveza**) or neutral (**lo bueno**). Generally, but not always, masculine words end in "o" and feminine in "a". To talk about more than one object, add "s" to words that conclude with a vowel and "es" after a consonant.

Words flow in an order similar to English, but adjectives tend to come after the words they describe: for example, **comida buena** versus "good food".

Spanish marks a question before and after the phrase – that distinctive mirrored punctuation:

¿Qué tal?   **¡Hola!**

Also, the ending of a verb indicates who is doing the action and when; **tomo** means "I take", while **tomaremos** is "we will take". A casual visitor doesn't need to memorise all the possibilities, just understand why a word can change from phrase to phrase.

Here's the most basic way to express an idea happening now. Take the infinitive – the "to X" form listed in a dictionary – and lop off the last two letters:

tom-ar	**com-er**	**part-ir**
to take	to eat	to leave

Now add the appropriate ending:

yo I	**tom-o** take	**com-o** eat	**part-o** leave
tú You	**tom-as** take	**com-es** eat	**part-es** leave
él, ella He/She	**tom-a** takes	**com-e** eats	**part-e** leaves
nosotros We	**tom-amos** take	**com-emos** eat	**part-imos** leave

vosotros	tom-áis	com-éis	part-ís
You	take	eat	leave

ellos, ellas	tom-an	com-en	part-en
They	take	eat	leave

Most importantly, don't let the grammar scare you. Yes, Spanish is an intricate, nuanced language, the tongue of Cervantes and other great poets. But it's also a very forgiving and user-friendly one at a basic level. And locals appreciate any attempt, especially when it's paired with a wide smile.

Basic conversation

Hello	Hola	_olah_
Goodbye	Adiós	_adyos_
Yes	Sí	_see_
No	No	_no_
Please	Por favor	_por fabor_
Thank you	Gracias	_grasyas_
You're welcome	De nada	_de nada_
Sorry	Perdón	_perdon_
Excuse me (apology)	Lo siento	_lo syento_
Excuse me (to get attention)	Perdone	_perdoneh_
Excuse me (to get past)	Con permiso	_kon permeeso_
Do you speak English?	¿Habla inglés?	_abla eengles?_
I don't speak Spanish	No hablo español	_no ablo espanyol_
I speak a little Spanish	Hablo un poco de español	_ablo oon poko de espanyol_
What?	¿Cómo dice?	_komo deese?_
I understand	Entiendo	_entyendo_
I don't understand	No entiendo	_no entyendo_
Do you understand?	¿Entiende?	_entyende?_
I don´t know	No sé	_no seh_
I can´t	No puedo	_no pwedo_
Can you...please?	¿Puede...por favor?	_pwede...por fabor?_
- speak more slowly	- hablar más despacio	- _ablar mas despasyo_
- repeat that	- repetirlo	- _repeteerlo_

Greetings

There are as many ways of saying
hello as there are countries in Latin
America. However, a simple ¡Hola!
or ¿Qué tál? will be understood
everywhere and will always earn
you a friendly smile and open up
previously closed doors. The **mundo
hispanoparlante** (Spanish-
speaking world) is made up of
around 400 million people, a fact
that doesn't really encourage Latin
Americans to learn other
languages. (Sound familiar?) Your
efforts to address locals in their own
language will therefore be much
appreciated in the larger cities, and
absolutely essential when visiting
more remote areas or villages!

Meeting someone

Hello	**Hola**	_o_lah
Hi	**Hola**	_o_lah
Good morning	**Buenos días**	_bwe_nos _dee_as
Good afternoon	**Buenas tardes**	_bwe_nas _tar_des
Good evening	**Buenas tardes**	_bwe_nas _tar_des
How are you?	**¿Cómo está?/**	_ko_mo es_tah_? /keh tal?
	¿Qué tál?	
Fine, thank you	**Bien, gracias**	byen, _gras_yas
And you?	**¿Y usted?**	ee oos_ted_?
Very well	**Muy bien**	mooy byen
Not very well	**No muy bien**	no mooy byen
Sir/Mr	**Señor/Sr**	sen_yor_/sen_yor_
Madam/Mrs	**Señora/Sra**	sen_yo_ra/sen_yo_ra
Miss	**Señorita**	senyo_ree_ta

Warm welcome
Meet your hosts with respect and – ideally – some Spanish words! They will accord you a most hearty welcome and offer their help where they can.

Small talk

My name is...	**Me llamo...**	me _ya_mo...
What's your name?	**¿Cómo se llama?**	_ko_mo se _ya_ma?
I'm pleased to meet you	**Encantado/a de conocerle/a**	enkan_ta_do/a de kono_ser_le/a

Where are you from?	¿De dónde es?	_de dondeh es?_
I am from Britain	Soy de Gran Bretaña	_soy de gran bretanya_
Do you live here?	¿Vive aquí?	_beebe akee?_
This is a great...	Este/a es... estupendo/a	_este/a es... estoopendo/a_
- country	- un país	- _oon pays_
- city/town	- una ciudad	- _oona seeoodad_
I am staying at...	Me hospedo en...	_me ospedo en..._
I'm just here for the day	Estoy aquí sólo para pasar el día	_estoy akee solo para pasar el deea_
I'm in... for...	Estoy en...por...	_estoy en...por..._
- a weekend	- un fin de semana	- _oon feen de semana_
- a week	- una semana	- _oona semana_
How old are you?	¿Cuántos años tiene?	_kwantos anyos tyene?_
I´m...years old	Tengo...años	_tengo...anyos_

Family

This is my...	Este/a es mi...	_este/a es mee..._
- husband	- esposo	- _esposo_
- wife	- esposa	- _esposa_
- partner	- pareja	- _pareha_
- boyfriend/ girlfriend	- novio/a	- _nobyo/a_
I have...	Tengo...	_tengo..._
- a son	- un hijo	- _oon eeho_
- a daughter	- una hija	- _oona eeha_
- a grandson	- un nieto	- _oon nyeto_
- a granddaughter	- una nieta	- _oona nyeta_
Do you have...	¿Tiene...	_tyene..._
- children?	- hijos?	_eehos?_
- grandchildren?	- nietos?	_nyetos?_
I don´t have children	No tengo hijos	_no tengo eehos_
Are you married?	¿Está casado/a?	_estah kasado/a?_

11

I'm...	Estoy...	estoy...
- single	- soltero/a	- soltero/a
- married	- casado/a	- kasado/a
- divorced	- divorciado/a	- deeborsyado/a
- widowed	- viudo/a	- byoodo/a

Saying goodbye

Goodbye	Adiós	adyos
Good night	Buenas noches	bwenas noches
Sleep well	Que duerma bien	ke dwerma byen
See you later	Hasta luego	asta lwego
Have a good trip	Buen viaje	bwen byahe
It was nice meeting you	Ha sido un placer conocerle/a	a seedo oon plaser konoserle/a
All the best	Que vaya todo bien	ke baya todo byen
Have fun	Páselo bien	paselo byen
Good luck	Buena suerte	bwena swerte
Keep in touch	Manténgase en contacto	mantengase en kontakto
My address is...	Mi dirección es...	mee dereksyon es...
What's your...	¿Cuál es su...	kwal es soo...
- address?	- dirección?	- dereksyon?
- email?	- correo electrónico?	- korreo elektroneeko?
- telephone number?	- número de teléfono?	- noomero de telephono?

All latinos, but still different...
Leave all your cliches behind and get to know a fascinating world beyond party, dancing and rum. However if you're invited: don't leave out a real **fiesta latina!!!**

Eating out

Throughout Latin America, one country's cuisine stands head and shoulders above the rest: Mexico. Its dishes offer unique flavours and artful combinations of ingredients such as chilli and chocolate. Others are similar, but none is as rich in variety and taste. Caribbean food, when it goes beyond rice, beans, chicken and plantains, is worth sampling; while Cuba is undergoing an unprecedented culinary revival as a result of the new and privately-run **paladares** restaurant scene.

Though the cuisines of each country in Latin America differ enormously, they do have one common denominator: meat! Vegetarians can console themselves with the sweetest tropical fruits available and an array of vegetable **entremeses** (starters) that are delicacies in their own right.

Introduction to food & drink

Before you start you should know that there are some different words used for the same things in different countries. In Mexico the word **tomate** refers to green tomatoes whereas the 'normal' tomato is called **jítomate**. Butter is **manteca** in South America and **mantequilla** everywhere else. But don't worry: the phrases below will get you along everywhere!

I'd like...	**Quisiera...**	*Keesyera...*
- a table for two	**- una mesa para dos**	*- oona mesa para dos*
- a soft drink	**- un refresco**	*- oon rephresko*
- a coffee (with milk)	**- un café (con leche)**	*- oon kapheh (kon leche)*
- a tea	**- un té**	*- oon the*
Do you have a menu in English?	**¿Tiene un menú en inglés?**	*tyene oon menoo en eengles?*
The bill, please	**La cuenta, por favor**	*la kwenta, por fabor*

You may hear...

¿Fumadores o no fumadores?	*phoomadores o no phoomadores?*	Smoking or non-smoking?
¿Qué va a tomar?	*keh ba a tomar?*	What are you going to have?

Latin American cuisines

The Caribbean
CUBA AND DOMINICAN REPUBLIC

Signature dishes
(see the Menu decoder for more dishes)

Picadillo a la habanera (Cuba)	*peekadeeyo a la habanera*	Minced meat in a tomato, pepper and olive sauce
Langosta Varadero (Cuba)	*langosta baradero*	Lobster in tomato, garlic and onion
Arroz con pollo (Cuba, Dom. Rep.)	*arros kon poyo*	Rice cooked with chicken and spices

Who loves seafood?

The Dominican Republic has the most wonderful dishes for seafood-lovers. **Mariscos** specialities include fish in coconut sauce, shrimp stew, cod a la Dominicana, stewed conch and stuffed crab.

Sancocho (Dom. Rep.)	*sankocho*	Spicy meat and vegetable stew
La bandera (Dom. Rep.)	*la bandera*	Rice, red beans, green plantains and meat (the colours of the flag)
Asopao de mariscos (Dom. Rep.)	*asopao de mareeskos*	Thick rice soup with seafood
Pastelones (Dom. Rep.)	*pastelones*	Pies filled with meat or cheese

Central America
MEXICO

Signature dishes
(see the Menu decoder for more dishes)

Huevos rancheros	*hwebos rancheros*	Fried eggs, tortilla and tomato sauce
Enchilada	*encheelada*	Tortilla filled with meat or cheese, baked, chilli sauce
Quesadilla	*kesadeeya*	Fried or baked cheese-filled tortilla
Taco al pastor	*tako al pastor*	Small tortilla with pork, coriander, onions, pineapple

¿Es picoso? (Is it hot?)

Remember this phrase: you'll need it in Mexican restaurants. If the answer is **um poco** (a little), be sure that your throat will still be burning by the time you leave.

Chile relleno	_chee_le re_ye_no	Deep-fried chilli pepper filled with meat or cheese
Chile en nogada	_chee_le en no_ga_da	Meat-filled chilli pepper, walnut sauce
Filete a la tampiqueña	phee_le_teh a la tam-pee_ke_nya	Tenderloin, usually with an enchilada

OTHER COUNTRIES

Signature dishes
(see the Menu decoder for more dishes)

Olla de carne (Costa Rica)	_o_ya de _kar_ne	Vegetable and meat soup
Tamales (Central America)	ta_ma_les	Steamed, filled corn dough in corn husks or banana leaves
Baleadas (Honduras)	bale_a_das	Tortilla filled with beans, chorizo, vegetables
Subanik (Guatemala)	soo_ba_neek	Beef, chicken and pork steamed in a spicy sauce
Pupusa (El Salvador)	poo_poo_sa	Corn or rice tortilla with beans, fish or vegetables
Carimañolas (Panama)	kareeman_yo_las	Manioc pies with various fillings

South America

Signature dishes
(see the Menu decoder for more dishes)

Asado (Argentina)	_a<u>sa</u>do_	Barbecue with steak, beef ribs and sausages
Pastel de choclo (Chile)	_pas<u>tel</u> de <u>cho</u>klo_	Meat and corn pie
Empanadas (Andean countries)	_empa<u>na</u>das_	Turnovers with a meat, cheese or vegetable filling
Humitas (Andean countries)	_hoo<u>mee</u>tas_	Filled corn dough, steamed in husks
Locro (Argentina, Chile, Bolivia)	_<u>lo</u>kro_	Stew with local ingredients (meats and corn grains)

Rare, medium or well done

Argentine beef is famous the world over and the **bife de lomo** is a very thick tenderloin fillet that you can almost cut with a spoon. Try it at least once in your lifetime!

Wine, beer & spirits

Choose ice-cold beer in the Caribbean and Central America: the wine served in average restaurants is just about passable. Local beers are good quality and suit the rather heavy and spicy food perfectly. In the evening, sipping cocktails is a good way to chill out and contemplate the day's adventures.

I'd like to try... **Quisiera probar...** _Kee<u>sye</u>ra pro<u>bar</u>..._
- a banana Daiquiri **- un banana daiquiri** _- oon ba<u>na</u>na day<u>kee</u>ree_

English	Spanish	Pronunciation
- a Margarita	- **una margarita**	- _oo_na marga_ree_ta
- an aged Tequila	- **un tequila añejo**	- oon te_kee_la a_nye_ho
- a pisco sour	- **un pisco sour**	- oon _pees_ko sour
- wine from Chile	- **un vino chileno**	- oon _bee_no chee_le_no
Could I have...	**¿Me pone...**	me _pone_...
- a beer?	- **una cerveza?**	- _oo_na ser_be_sa?
- a glass/a bottle of white/red/ rosé wine?	- **un vaso/una botella de vino blanco/tinto/ rosado?**	- oon _ba_so/_oo_na bo_te_ya de _bee_no _blan_ko/_teen_to/ ro_sa_do?
- a glass/a bottle of champagne?	- **una copa/una botella de champán?**	- _oo_na _ko_pa/_oo_na bo_te_lla de cham_pan_?
- a gin and tonic?	- **un gin tonic?**	- oon heen _to_neek?
- a Cuba Libre?	- **un cuba libre?**	- oon _koo_ba _lee_bre?
- a whisky?	- **un güisqui?**	- oon _bees_kee?

Cocteles	kok_te_les	Cocktails
Margarita	marga_ree_ta	Tequila and lime juice
Mojito	mo_hee_to	Rum, lime juice, sugar and mint leaves
Cuba libre	_koo_ba _lee_bre	White rum and cola
Cubata	koo_ba_ta	Dark rum and cola
Daiquiri	day_kee_ree	Rum and lime on crushed ice
Piña colada	_pee_nya ko_la_da	Rum, cream, pineapple and coconut

Hemingway's bar

The Floridita was Hemingway's favourite hangout in Havana and it hasn't changed a whole lot since. The poet is still holding up the bar at his favourite stool – join him for a Daiquiri!

How to eat cactus

The cactus (**nopal**) does not just adorn the Mexican landscape. You'll find it at the centre of tasty dishes such as salads and stews. The sweet fruit, called **tuna**, is also worth a try!

You may hear...

¿Qué le pongo?	keh le <u>pon</u>go?	What can I get you?
¿Cómo lo quiere?	komo lo <u>kye</u>re?	How would you like it?
¿Con o sin hielo?	kon o seen <u>ye</u>lo?	With or without ice?
¿Frío/a o natural?	<u>free</u>o/a o natoo<u>ral</u>?	Cold or room temperature?

Snacks & refreshments

There's no doubt about it, some of the best and most authentic local food can be found in the tiny street stands you'll see everywhere. It's tempting to try, but choose your meal carefully: some can be harmful for European stomachs! Savour the Argentine version of a burger, the **lomito**: bread with a tender and juicy beef fillet!

Sándwich	<u>sand</u>weech	Sandwich
Perro caliente	<u>perro</u> kal<u>yen</u>te	Hot Dog
Hamburguesa (con queso)	hamboor<u>ge</u>sa (kon <u>ke</u>so)	Hamburger (cheeseburger)
Empanadas	empa<u>na</u>das	Turnovers with various fillings
Antojitos mexicanos	anto<u>hee</u>tos mehee<u>ka</u>nos	Mexican snacks (tacos, tamales...)
Medianoche (Cuba)	medya<u>no</u>che	Ham and cheese sandwich with tomato, pickles and mayonnaise
Pastelitos (Dom. Rep.)	paste<u>lee</u>tos	Pastry meat or cheese turnovers

Chimichurri (Dom. Rep.)	*cheemee<u>choo</u>ree*	Typical pork sandwich
Arreglados (Costa Rica)	*arre<u>gla</u>dos*	Meat and vegetable sandwich
Lomito (Argentina)	*lo<u>mee</u>to*	Beef, ham, cheese, tomato and lettuce sandwich

Vegetarians & special requirements

I'm vegetarian	**Soy vegetariano/a**	*soy behetar<u>ya</u>no/a*
I don't eat...	**No como...**	*no <u>ko</u>mo...*
- meat	**- carne**	*- <u>kar</u>ne*
- fish	**- pescado**	*- pes<u>ka</u>do*
Could you cook something without meat in it?	**¿Me pueden preparar algo sin carne?**	*me <u>pwe</u>den prepa<u>rar</u> algo seen <u>kar</u>ne?*
What's in this?	**¿Qué lleva esto?**	*keh <u>ye</u>ba <u>es</u>to?*
I'm allergic...	**Tengo alergia...**	*tengo a<u>ler</u>hya...*
- to nuts	**- a los frutos secos**	*- a los <u>phroo</u>tos <u>se</u>kos*
- to gluten	**- al gluten**	*- al <u>gloo</u>ten*
- to dairy	**- a los productos lácteos**	*- a los pro<u>dook</u>tos <u>lak</u>teos*

Children

Are children welcome?	**¿Admiten niños?**	*ad<u>mee</u>ten <u>neen</u>yos?*
Do you have a children's menu?	**¿Tienen menú para niños?**	*<u>tye</u>nen me<u>noo</u> para <u>neen</u>yos?*
What dishes are good for children?	**¿Qué platos son buenos para niños?**	*keh <u>pla</u>tos son <u>bwe</u>nos para <u>neen</u>yos?*

Coffee in Costa Rica...
...is a home-grown thing, produced in seven regions located in the lowlands and highlands. Here coffee is not just coffee, but a delicacy of seven different flavours.

Essentials

Breakfast	**El desayuno**	*el desayoono*
Lunch	**El almuerzo**	*el almooerso*
Dinner	**La cena**	*la sena*
Snack	**La merienda**	*la meryenda*
Cover charge	**El precio del cubierto**	*el presyo del koobyerto*
Vat inclusive	**IVA incluido**	*eeba eenklooeedo*
Service included	**Servicio incluido**	*serbeeseeo eenklooeedo*
Credit cards (not) accepted	**(No) aceptamos tarjetas de crédito**	*(no) aseptamos tarhettas de kredeeto*
First course	**El primer plato**	*el preemer plato*
Second course	**El segundo plato**	*el segoondo plato*
Dessert	**El postre**	*el postre*
Dish of the day	**El plato del día**	*el plato del deea*
House specials	**Las especialidades de la casa**	*las espeseealeedades de la kasa*
Set menu	**El menú del día**	*el menoo del deea*
A la carte menu	**El menú a la carta**	*el menoo a la karta*
Tourist menu	**El menú turista**	*el menoo tooreesta*
Wine list	**La carta de vinos**	*la karta de beenos*
Drinks menu	**El menú de bebidas**	*el menoo de bebeedas*

Methods of preparation

Baked	**Al horno**	*al orno*
Boiled	**Cocido/a**	*koseedo/a*
Braised	**Cocinado/a a fuego lento**	*koseenado/a a phwego lento*
Breaded	**Rebozado/a**	*rebosado/a*
Deep-fried	**Frito/a en mucho aceite**	*phreeto/a en moocho aseyte*
Fresh	**Fresco/a**	*phresko/a*
Fried	**Frito/a**	*phreeto/a*
Frozen	**Congelado/a**	*konhelado/a*
Grilled/broiled	**A la parrilla**	*a la pareeya*
Marinated	**En adobo**	*en adobo*

Chillis, chillis, chillis

Chilli peppers are a science unto themselves in Mexico. You can find **chile poblano**, **chile jalapeño**, **chile habanero**, **chile serrano**, and many more, each variety distinguished by its colour and the degree of hotness.

Mashed	**En puré**	*en pooreh*
Poached	**Escalfado/a**	*eskalphado/a*
Raw	**Crudo/a**	*kroodo/a*
Roasted	**Asado/a**	*asado/a*
Salty	**Salado/a**	*salado/a*
Sautéed	**Salteado/a**	*salteado/a*
Smoked	**Ahumado/a**	*aoomado/a*
Spicy (flavour)	**Condimentado/a**	*kondeementado/a*
Spicy (hot)	**Picante**	*peekante*
Steamed	**Al vapor**	*al bapor*
Stewed	**Estofado/a**	*estophado/a*
Stuffed	**Relleno/a**	*reyeno/a*
Sweet	**Dulce**	*doolse*
Rare	**Poco hecho/a**	*normal*
Medium	**Normal**	*poko echo/a*
Well done	**Bien hecho/a**	*byen echo/a*

Common food items

Beef	**La carne de res**	*la karne de res*
Chicken	**El pollo**	*el poyo*
Turkey	**El pavo**	*el pabo*
Lamb	**El cordero**	*el kordero*
Pork	**La carne de cerdo**	*la karne de serdo*
Fish	**El pescado**	*el peskado*
Seafood	**El marisco**	*el mareesko*
Crab	**El cangrejo**	*el kangreho*
Prawn	**El camarón**	*el kamaron*
Lobster	**La langosta**	*la langosta*
Tuna	**El atún**	*el atoon*

Beans	**Los frijoles**	*los phreeholes*
Cheese	**El queso**	*el keso*
Eggs	**Los huevos**	*los ooebos*
Lentils	**Las lentejas**	*las lentehas*
Pasta/noodles	**La pasta/los fideos**	*la pasta/los pheedeos*
Rice	**El arroz**	*el arros*

Avocado	**El aguacate**	*el agwakate*
Cabbage	**La berza**	*la bersa*
Carrots	**Las zanahorias**	*las sanaoreeas*
Corn	**El maíz**	*el maees*
Corn (Central America)	**El elote**	*el elote*
Cucumber	**El pepino**	*el pepeeno*
Garlic	**El ajo**	*el aho*
Manioc	**La yuca**	*la yooka*
Mushrooms	**Los champiñones**	*los champeenyones*
Olives	**Las aceitunas**	*las aseytoonas*
Onion	**La cebolla**	*la seboya*
Potato	**La papa**	*la papa*
Pumpkin	**La calabaza**	*la kalabasa*
Red/green pepper	**El pimiento rojo/verde**	*el peemyento roho/berde*
Sweet potato	**El boniato**	*el bonyato*
Tomato	**El tomate**	*el tomate*
Vegetables	**Las verduras**	*las berdooras*

Bread	**El pan**	*el pan*
Oil	**El aceite**	*el aseyte*
Pepper	**La pimienta**	*la peemyenta*

Salt	**La sal**	*la sal*
Vinegar	**El vinagre**	*el bee<u>na</u>gre*
Cake	**El pastel**	*el pas<u>tel</u>*
Cereal	**Los cereales**	*los sere<u>a</u>les*
Cream	**La nata/crema**	*la <u>na</u>ta/<u>kre</u>ma*
Fruit	**La fruta**	*la <u>phroo</u>ta*
Ice-cream	**El helado**	*el e<u>la</u>do*
Milk	**La leche**	*la <u>leche</u>*
Tart	**La tarta**	*la <u>tar</u>ta*

Popular sauces

Guacamole (Mexico)	*gwaka<u>mole</u>*	Avocado, coriander and chilli
Mole (Mexico)	*<u>mo</u>le*	Spicy chilli and dark chocolate
Salsa mexicana (Mexico)	*<u>sal</u>sa mehee<u>ka</u>na*	Diced tomatoes, onions, coriander and chilli
Salsa roja (Mexico)	*<u>sal</u>sa <u>ro</u>ha*	Hot and spicy tomato sauce
Salsa verde (Mexico)	*<u>sal</u>sa <u>ber</u>de*	Hot and spicy green tomato
Salsa criolla (Cuba and Central America)	*<u>sal</u>sa kree<u>oy</u>a*	Spiced olive oil, tomato, garlic and onion
Chimichurri (Argentina)	*cheemee<u>choo</u>ree*	Parsley and garlic

Get married at lunch time
Costa Rica's typical lunch dish is the **casado** (married).
It is composed of rice, black beans, meat, fried plantains
and a cabbage and tomato salad. If only you'd known
proposing would be this easy!

First course dishes

Crema de queso (Cuba)	_krema de keso_	Creamy cheese soup
Sopa de pescado (Dom. Rep.)	_sopa de peskado_	Fish soup
Quipes (Dom. Rep.)	_keepes_	Deep-fried bulgur rolls with minced meat
Ensalada de nopal (Mexico)	_ensalada de nopal_	Avocado, tomato, onion and nopal cactus salad
Crema de elote (Mexico)	_krema de elote_	Creamy corn cream
Sopa de tortilla (Mexico)	_sopa de torteeya_	Chilli, tomato and onion soup topped with tortilla slices and cheese
Sopa negra (Costa Rica)	_sopa negra_	Black bean soup
Sopa de mondongo (Costa Rica, Nicaragua)	_sopa de mondongo_	Tripe and vegetable soup
Ceviche (Central America)	_sebeeche_	Marinated seafood starter
Caldo de pollo (Argentina)	_kaldo de poyo_	Chicken soup
Croquetas de arroz (Argentina)	_krokettas de arros_	Rice croquettes

Second course dishes

Ropa vieja (Cuba)	_ropa byeha_	Shredded beef in spicy tomato sauce ('old clothes')
Chivo picante (Dom. Rep.)	_cheebo peekante_	Spicy goat meat stew
Lambi guisado (Dom. Rep.)	_lambee geesado_	Conch stew
Pozole (Mexico)	_posoleh_	Spicy dried corn, pork and chilli stew
Mole poblano (Mexico)	_mole poblano_	Turkey in Mole chocolate sauce
Cochinita pibil (Mexico)	_kocheeneeta pee-beel_	Pork in banana leaves baked in earth oven
Arroz con tuna/ pollo (Costa Rica)	_arros kon toona/ poyo_	Rice with tuna or chicken

Home-made and authentic

The **paladares** – Cuba's private restaurants – are the best place for tasting authentic Cuban food. Don't look for them in your guidebook, however, but ask a local to recommend a good one: **¿Me puede recomendar un paladare bueno?**

Tilapia (Costa Rica)	*teelapeeya*	Fish with garlic and lime juice
Gallina rellena (Nicaragua)	*gayeena reyena*	Chicken stuffed with herbs and vegetables
Bife de lomo a la plancha (Argentina)	*beefe de lomo a la plancha*	Grilled tenderloin steak
Cazuela de ave (Chile)	*kasooela de abe*	Chicken, potato, rice and green pepper stew
Parillada (Bolivia)	*pareeyada*	Mixed grill with offal and intestines

Side dishes

Congrí (Cuba)	*kongree*	Rice cooked with red beans
Moros y Cristianos (Cuba)	*moros ee kreesteeanos*	Rice with black beans ('Moors and Christians')
Tostones de plátano (Cuba, Dom. Rep.)	*tostones de platano*	Fried plantain slices
Frijoles refritos (Mexico)	*phreeholes rephreetos*	Typical bean paste
Totopos (Mexico)	*totopos*	Tortilla chips

Gallo pinto (Central America)	*gayo peento*	Rice with black beans ('Spotted Rooster')
Patacones (Costa Rica)	*patakones*	Thin slices of deep-fried plantain
Ensalada criolla (Argentina)	*ensalada kreeoya*	Cabbage, apple and walnut salad
Patatas fritas	*patatas phreetas*	Chips
Puré de patatas	*pooreh de patatas*	Mashed potatoes
Guarnición	*gwarneethyon*	Vegetables
Ensalada	*ensalada*	Salad

Desserts

Arroz con leche	*arros kon leche*	Rice pudding
Flan	*flan*	Crème caramel
Dulce de leche	*doolse de leche*	Caramel cream
Ensalada de fruta	*ensalada de phroota*	Fruit salad
Helados variados	*elados bareeados*	Ice-cream (several flavours)
Tarta de queso	*tarta de keso*	Cheesecake
Natilla	*nateeya*	Custard in various local variations

Drinks

Café con leche	*kapheh kon leche*	Coffee with milk
Café solo/negro	*kapheh solo/negro*	Black coffee
Chocolate	*chokolatte*	Hot chocolate
Descafeinado (con leche)	*deskapheynado (kon leche)*	Decaffeinated coffee (with milk)
Infusión	*eenphoosyon*	Herbal tea
Té (con leche/limón)	*te (kon leche/leemon)*	Tea (with milk/lemon)
Agua mineral sin/con gas	*agwa meeneral seen/kon gas*	Still/sparkling mineral water
Jugo de naranja	*hoogo de naranha*	Orange juice
Jugo natural	*hoogo natooral*	Fresh fruit juice
Cerveza/cerveza de barril	*serbesa/serbesa de barreel*	Beer/draught beer
Cola	*kola*	Cola
Refrescos	*rephreskos*	Soft drinks
Vino blanco/tinto /rosado	*beeno blanko/teento/rosado*	White/red/rosé wine

27

Cocteles	*kokteles*	Cocktails
Margarita	*margareeta*	Tequila and lime juice
Mojito	*moheeto*	Rum, lime juice, sugar, mint leaves
Cuba libre	*kooba leebre*	White rum and cola
Cubata	*koobata*	Dark rum and cola
Daiquiri	*daykeeree*	Rum and lime on crushed ice
Piña colada	*peenya kolada*	Rum, pineapple, cream, coconut

Fruits & nuts

Almond	**La almendra**	*la almendra*
Apple	**La manzana**	*la mansana*
Banana	**La banana**	*la banana*
Cherry	**La cereza**	*la seresa*
Coconut	**El coco**	*el coco*
Custard apple	**La Guanábana**	*la gwanabana*
Fig	**El higo**	*el eego*
Guava	**La guayaba**	*la gwayaba*
Grapefruit	**La toronja**	*la toronha*
Grapes	**Las uvas**	*las oobas*
Hazelnut	**La avellana**	*la abeyana*
Lemon	**El limón**	*el leemon*
Mamey	**El mamey**	*el mamey*
Mango	**El mango**	*el mango*
Melon	**El melón**	*el melon*
Orange	**La naranja**	*la naranha*
Papaya	**La papaya**	*la papaya*
Peach	**El melocotón**	*el melokoton*

Peruvian fast food

The Peruvian shish kebab variant is the **anticucho**, made with pieces of marinated beef heart. This is a typical local fast food: you can find it everywhere and at all hours of the day.

Shopping

The Caribbean – as well as Central and South America – is certainly more attractive for its beaches and cultural heritage than for its shopping. Yet the colourful street markets contain treasures, including **artesanías** (handicrafts).

Shops and stands also sell these local artworks, usually near historic city centres. Head in the opposite direction – towards the chic residential **barrios** – for modern shopping malls and designer boutiques.

Essentials

Where can I buy...?	¿Dónde puedo comprar...?	*dondeh pwedo komprar...?*
I'd like to buy...	Me gustaría comprar...	*me goostareea komprar...*
Do you sell...?	¿Venden...?	*benden...?*
I'd like this	Quiero esto	*kyero esto*
I'd prefer...	Preferiría...	*prephereereea...*
Could you show me...?	¿Me podría enseñar...?	*me podreea ensenyar...?*
I'm just looking, thanks	Sólo estoy mirando, gracias	*solo estoy meerando, grasyas*
How much is it?	¿Cuánto cuesta?	*kwanto kwesta?*
Could you write down the price?	¿Puede escribir el precio?	*pwede eskreebeer el presyo?*
Do you have any items on sale?	¿Tienen algo rebajado?	*tyenen algo rebahado?*
Could I have a discount?	¿Me puede hacer un descuento?	*me pwede aser oon deskwento?*
Nothing else, thanks	Nada más, gracias	*nada mas, grasias*
Do you accept credit cards?	¿Aceptan tarjetas de crédito?	*aseptan tarhettas de kredeeto?*
Could you post it to...?	¿Lo pueden enviar a...?	*lo pweden enbyar a...?*
Can I exchange it?	¿Puedo cambiarlo/a?	*pwedo kambyarlo/a?*
I'd like to return this	Quisiera devolver esto	*keesyera debolber esto*
I'd like a refund	¿Me puede devolver el dinero?	*me pwede debolber el deenero*

Local specialities

Tourist traps abound. Look closely to distinguish quality handcrafted products from cheap mass souvenirs. A hint: buy directly from the artist, avoiding intermediaries, who pad the cost.

Can you recommend a shop selling local specialities?	¿Me puede recomendar una tienda de productos típicos de la región?	*me pwede rekomendar oona tyenda de prodooktos teepeekos de la reheeon?*

Mamajuana (Dom. Rep.)	*mamahwana*	Liqueur made of rum, honey, herbs and spices
Joyas de ámbar y larimar (Dom. Rep.)	*hoyas de ambar ee lareemar*	Handcrafted jewellery made from amber and larimar stone

CENTRAL AMERICA

Tequila (Mexico)	*tekeela*	Drink extracted from the heart of the blue agave
Joyería de plata de Taxco (Mexico)	*hoyereea de plata de tassko*	Silver jewellery from Taxco
Cerámica Talavera de Puebla (Mexico)	*serameeka talabera de pwebla*	Hand-painted ceramics from Puebla
Artesanía de Sarchí (Costa Rica)	*artesaneea de sarchee*	Crafts from Sarchí, the cradle of Costa Rican art handicraft
Café de Costa Rica	*kapheh de kosta reeka*	High altitude organic coffee
Palo de lluvia (Guatemala)	*palo de yoobeea*	Bamboo stick used as a music instrument

SOUTH AMERICA

Juego de mate y bombilla (Argentina)	*hwego de mate ee bombeeya*	Mate tea set, usually made of a pumpkin and a metal straw
Poncho (Peru, Bolivia)	*poncho*	Hand-knitted poncho made of Alpaca wool
Charango (Chile, Peru, Bolivia)	*charango*	10-string miniature guitar

The silver city

Taxco was once an important mining centre. Today the colonial Mexican town attracts visitors with handmade silver jewellery.

Joyas de lapislázuli (Chile)	*hoyas de lapeesla-soolee*	Handcrafted lapis lazuli jewellery

Clothes & shoes

Where is the... department?	**¿Dónde está el departamento de...**	*dondeh estah el departamento de...*
- clothes	**- ropa?**	*- ropa?*
- shoe	**- zapatería?**	*- sapatereea?*
- women's	**- damas?**	*- damas?*
- men's	**- caballeros?**	*- kabayeros?*
- children's	**- niños?**	*- neenyos?*

Siesta in a hammock

In Central America, descendants of the Maya have preserved their weaving skill. Today, they craft comfortable hammocks, known as **hamacas**.

Which floor is the...?	**¿En qué piso está el/la...?**	*en keh peeso estah el/la...?*
I'm looking for...	**Estoy buscando...**	*estoy booskando...*
- a skirt	**- una falda**	*- oona falda*
- trousers	**- unos pantalones**	*- oonos pantalones*
- a top	**- un top**	*- oon top*
- a jacket	**- una chaqueta**	*- oona chaketta*
- a T-shirt	**- una camiseta**	*- oona kameesetta*
- jeans	**- unos jeans**	*- oonos dcheens*
- shoes	**- unos zapatos**	*- oonos sapatos*
- underwear	**- ropa interior**	*- ropa eenteryor*
Can I try it on?	**¿Puedo probármelo/a?**	*pwedo probarme-lo/a?*
What size is it?	**¿Qué talla es?**	*keh taya es?*

My size is...	Uso la talla...	*uso la taya...*
- small	- pequeña	- pekenya
- medium	- mediana	- medeeana
- large	- grande	- grande
Do you have this in my size?	¿Tienen esto en mi talla?	tyenen esto en mee taya?
Where is the changing room?	¿Dónde está el probador?	dondeh estah el probador?

It doesn't fit	No me sirve	*no me seerbe*
It doesn't suit me	No me queda bien	no me keda byen
Do you have a... size?	¿Tienen una talla...	tyenen oona taya...
- bigger	- mayor?	- mayor?
- smaller	- más pequeña?	- mas pekenya?

Do you have it/them in...	¿Lo/la(s) tienen en...	*lo/la(s) tyenen en...*
- black?	- negro/a?	- negro/a?
- white?	- blanco/a?	- blanko/a?
- blue?	- azul?	- asool?
- green?	- verde?	- berde?
- red?	- rojo/a?	- roho/a?

I'm going to leave it/them	Lo/la(s) voy a dejar	*lo/la(s) boy a dehar*
I'll take it / them	Me lo/la(s) llevo	me lo/la(s) yebo

Indigenous art

Folk art ranges from cheap-and-cheerful to museum quality. Taking home trinkets isn't a problem, but artworks may require extensive customs forms – and even an expert's opinion that the piece isn't a stolen antiquity.

Cocktail ingredients

Tequila, mescal and rum all make superb souvenirs (when permitted onboard airplanes). Look for the word **"añejo"** (aged) on the bottle; the older it is, the finer the quality.

You may hear...

¿Puedo ayudarle?	*pwedo ayoodarle?*	Can I help you?
¿Le atienden?	*le atyenden?*	Have you been served?
¿De qué tamaño?	*de keh tamanyo?*	What size?
No tenemos	*no tenemos*	We don't have any
Aquí tiene	*akee tyene*	Here you are
¿Algo más?	*algo mas?*	Anything else?
Son... (cincuenta) pesos	*son... (seenkwenta) pesos*	It´s... (50) pesos
Está rebajado/a	*estah rebahado/a*	It's reduced

Where to shop

Street markets peddle most objects found in stores. Expect cheap prices, inferior quality and bargaining excitement. Rehearse your lines and watch your opponents' strategies before plunging into the fray.

Where can I find a...	¿Dónde hay...	*dondeh ai...*
- a bookshop?	- una librería?	- *oona leebrereea?*
- a clothes shop?	- una tienda de ropa?	- *oona tyenda de ropa?*
- a department store?	- unos grandes almacenes?	- *oonos grandes almasenes?*
- a gift shop?	- una tienda de regalos?	- *oona tyenda de regalos?*
- a music shop?	- una tienda de música?	- *oona tyenda de mooseeka?*
- a market?	- un mercado?	- *oon merkado?*

- a newsagent?	**- un quiosco?**	- oon _keeosko_?
- a shoe shop?	**- una zapatería?**	- _oona_ sapate_reea_?
- a stationer's?	**- una papelería?**	- _oona_ papele_reea_?
- a souvenir shop?	**- una tienda de recuerdos?**	- _oona_ _tyen_da de rek_wer_dos?
What's the best place to buy...?	**¿Cuál es el mejor lugar para comprar...?**	kwal es el me_hor_ loo_gar_ _para_ com_prar_...?
I'd like to buy...	**Quisiera comprar...**	kees_ye_ra kom_prar_...
- a film	**- un rollo de fotos**	- oon _royo_ de _photos_
- an English newspaper	**- un periódico inglés**	- oon per_yo_deeko een_gles_
- a map	**- un mapa**	- oon _mapa_
- postcards	**- postales**	- post_ales_
- a present	**- un regalo**	- oon re_ga_lo
- stamps	**- sellos**	- _seyos_
- sun cream	**- loción solar**	- lo_syon_ so_lar_

Food & markets

Is there a supermarket/ market nearby?	**¿Hay un supermercado/ mercado cerca?**	ai oon soopermer_ka_do/m er_ka_do _ser_ka?
Can I have...	**¿Me pone...**	me _pone_...
- some bread?	**- pan?**	- pan?
- some fruit?	**- fruta?**	- _phroo_ta?
- some cheese?	**- queso?**	- _ke_so?
- a bottle of water?	**- una botella de agua?**	- _oona_ bo_teya_ de _agwa_?

The smell of the guava

Feast your senses at a fruit market. Stands overflow with guava, papaya, pineapple and other tropical delights. Be careful not to overindulge, though. Many cases of the **turistas** - dodgy tummies - are sparked by carnivores who devour eight times their normal fruit intake.

Getting around

Flights to Latin America have become a lot cheaper with the no-frills airline boom. Rates do fluctuate with the season, however. Around Christmas and the New Year, tickets are more expensive and harder to book.

Local carriers vary in price, levels of service and standards of safety. Modern inter-urban buses are a good alternative. They usually feature toilets, air-conditioning and a video screen. Trains, on the other hand, are probably the cheapest transport in Latin America, but offer little comfort.

Arrival

Non-stop flights connect many capital cities and tourist hotspots directly to Europe. Watch your luggage carefully at airports and bus terminals: magnets for thieves and hustlers. Seek out information desks, taxi queues – even advice from uniformed police – rather than help or services volunteered by a stranger.

Where is/are...	¿Dónde está/están...	dondeh estah/estan...
- the luggage from flight...?	- el equipaje del vuelo...?	- el ekeepahe del bwelo...?
- the luggage trolleys?	- los carros de equipaje?	- los karros de ekeepahe?
- the lost luggage office?	- la oficina de equipaje perdido?	- la opheeseena de ekeepahe perdeedo?

Where is/are...	¿Dónde está/están...	dondeh estah/estan...
- the buses?	- los autobuses?	- los awtobooses?
- the trains?	- los trenes?	- los trenes?
- the taxis?	- los taxis?	- los taksees?
- the car rental?	- la oficina de alquiler de carros?	- la opheeseena de alkeeler de karros?
- the exit?	- la salida?	- la saleeda?
How do I get to hotel...?	¿Cómo se va al hotel...?	komo se ba al otel...?

My baggage...	Mi equipaje...	mee ekeepahe...
- is lost	- se ha extraviado	- se a ekstrabeeado
- is damaged	- está roto	- estaH roto
My baggage is stolen	Me han robado mi equipaje	me an robado mee ekeepahe

Customs

The children are on this passport	Los niños están en este pasaporte	los neenyos estan en este pasaporteh
We're here on holiday	Estamos acá de vacaciones	estamos akah de vakasyones
I'm going to...	Voy a...	boy a...
I have nothing to declare	No tengo nada que declarar	no tengo nada ke deklarar

| Do I have to declare this? | ¿Tengo que declarar esto? | *tengo ke declarar esto?* |

Car hire

The Motorcycle Diaries captured the thrills and chills of Latin American road trips. Driving can be a risky endeavour there. Should you take the plunge, research local customs, as well as recommended routes and equipment before booking. A brand-name hire agency may be worth the money.

I'd like to hire...	**Me gustaría alquilar...**	*me goostareea alkeelar...*
- a car	**- un carro**	*- oon karro*
- a people carrier	**- un mono-volumen**	*- oon mono boloomen*
with...	**con...**	*kon...*
- air conditioning	**- aire acondicionado**	*- ayre akondeesyonado*
- automatic transmission	**- transmisión automática**	*- tranmeeseeon awtomateeka*
How much is that for...	**¿Cuánto cuesta por...**	*kwanto kwesta por...*
- a day?	**- un día?**	*- oon deea?*
- a week?	**- una semana?**	*- oona semana?*
Does that include...	**¿Incluye el...**	*eenklooye el...*
- mileage?	**- kilometraje?**	*- keelometrahe?*
- insurance?	**- seguro?**	*- segooro?*

On the road

Strong nerves are helpful, when navigating major Latin American cities. Expect fast, aggressive traffic and exuberant honking. As a rule, toll roads are better and safer than free highways.

What is the speed limit?	¿Cuál es el límite de velocidad?	*kwal es el leemeete de beloseedad?*
Can I park here?	¿Puedo aparcar acá?	*pwedo aparkar akah?*
Where is a petrol station?	¿Dónde está la gasolinera?	*dondeh estah la gasoleenera?*

Please fill up the tank with...	**Por favor lléneme el depósito con gasolina...**	*por fabor yeneme el deposeeto kon gasoleena...*
- unleaded	**- sin plomo**	*- sin plomo*
- diesel	**- dizel**	*- dyesel*
- leaded	**- con plomo**	*- kon plomo*

Directions

Is this the road to...?	**¿Es esta la carretera a...?**	*es esta la karretera a...?*
How do I get to...?	**¿Cómo se va a...?**	*komo se ba a...?*
How far is it to...?	**¿Qué distancia hay a...?**	*keh deestansya ai a...?*
How long will it take to...?	**¿Cuánto se tarda a...?**	*kwanto se tarda a...?*
Could you point it out on the map?	**¿Me puede indicar dónde está en el mapa?**	*me pwede een-deekar dondeh estah en el mapa?*
I've lost my way	**Me he perdido**	*me eh perdeedo*
On the right/left	**A la derecha/ izquierda**	*ah la derecha/ eeskyerda*
Turn right/left	**Gire a la derecha/ izquierda**	*heere a la derecha/ eeskyerda*
Straight ahead	**Todo recto**	*todo rekto*
Turn around	**De la vuelta**	*de la bwelta*

Public transport

The common term for "bus" changes from country to country: **el camello** (Cuba), **el camión** (Mexico), **la chiva** (Colombia), **la guagua** (Cuba, Peru), **la góndola** (Chile, Colombia), **el collectivo** (Argentina, Peru, Venezuela). Whatever you call them, follow one common rule: watch your pockets, especially when boarding.

Bus	**El autobús**	*el awtoboos*
Bus station	**La estación de autobuses**	*la estasyon de awto-booses*
Train	**El tren**	*el tren*
Train station	**La estación de trenes**	*la estasyon de trenes*
Ferry	**El ferry**	*el feree*
Ferry port	**El puerto**	*el pwerto*
I'd like to go to...	**Quisiera ir a...**	*keesyera eer ah...*

The world's highest train

The **Ferrocarril Central** climbs to 5,000 meters en route from Lima to Huancayo. Relax onboard and watch the Peruvian sierra unfold.

I'd like a...ticket	**Quisiera un boleto...**	*keesyera oon boleto...*
- single	**- de ida/de viaje sencillo**	*- de eeda/de beeahe senceeyo*
- return	**- de ida y vuelta/de viaje redondo**	*- de eeda ee vuelta/de beeahe redondo*
- first-class	**- de primera clase**	*- de preemera klase*
- smoking/non-smoking	**- fumador/no-fumador**	*- foohmador/no-foohmador*
What time does it leave/arrive?	**¿A qué hora sale/llega?**	*a keh ora sale/yega?*
Could you tell me when to get off?	**¿Me puede indicar cuándo me bajo?**	*me pwede eendeekar kwando me baho?*

Taxis

Don't leave home without learning to say **¿Funciona el taxímetro?** If the driver says no (and the chances of this are high) then settle on the fare in advance. Be aware that in some countries bogus taxi drivers are common!

I'd like a taxi to...	**Quisiera un taxi para ir a...**	*keesyera oon taksee para eer a...*
Does the taximeter work?	**¿Funciona el taxímetro?**	*foonseeona el takseemetro?*
How much is it to the...	**¿Cuánto cuesta al...**	*kwanto kwesta al...*

- airport?	**- aeropuerto?**	_- aeropwerto?_
- town centre?	**- centro?**	_- sentro?_
- hotel...?	**- hotel...?**	_- otel...?_

Tours

Soft adventure tours are gaining popularity in Latin America: trekking in the jungle, float trips, horseback tours, etc. More daring guests can paraglide over turquoise bays or dive below with sharks.

Are there any organised tours of the town/region?	**¿Hay excursiones guiadas de la ciudad/región?**	_ai ekskoorsyones gyadas de la syoodad/rehyon?_
Where do they leave from?	**¿De dónde salen?**	_de dondeh salen?_
What time does it start?	**¿A qué hora empieza?**	_a keh ora empyesa?_
Do you have English-speaking guides?	**¿Tienen guías que hablan inglés?**	_tyenen gyas ke ablan eengles?_

Close to the deities

Mexico's Yucatan Peninsula is home to the most impressive Mayan temples and pyramids. These pre-Columbian sites still resonate with mystery and power.

Accommodation

Despite the usual array of hotels, many travellers prefer guesthouses – **casas de huéspedes** – for both price and atmosphere. Ecotourism resorts serve a similar role in Central America.

Mexico shelters guests in **cabañas**, palm-roofed huts, as well as rustic country homes.

The Cuban B&B is the **casa particular** (a room for rent in a private home). Don't expect much comfort, but enjoy the authentic lifestyle.

Types of accommodation

Hotels remain popular, but apartments – equipped with full kitchens – are increasingly attractive, especially for those concerned about food hygiene. Splash out on a jungle lodge in Costa Rica or a luxury villa in the Dominican Republic, complete with a concierge and personal chef.

I'd like to stay in...	**Quisiera alojarme en...**	keesyera aloharme en...
- an apartment	**- un apartamento**	- oon apartamento
- a campsite	**- un camping**	- oon kamping
- a hotel	**- un hotel**	- oon otel
- an apart-hotel	**- un apart-hotel**	- oon apart-otel
- a youth hostel	**- un albergue juvenil**	- oon alberge hoobeneel
- a guest house	**- una pension/una casa de huéspedes**	- oona pensyon/ oona kasa de hwespedes

Is it...	**¿Es...**	es...
- full board?	**- pensión completa?**	- pensyon kompletta?
- half board?	**- media pensión?**	- medya pensyon?
- self-catering?	**- sin servicio de comidas?**	- seen serbeesyo de komeedas?

Reservations

Do you have any rooms available?	**¿Tienen habitaciones libres?**	tyenen abeetasyones leebres?
Can you recommend anywhere else?	**¿Me puede recomendar otro sitio?**	me pwede rekomendar otro seetyo?
I'd like to make a reservation for...	**Quiero hacer una reserva para...**	kyero ather oona reserba para...
- tonight	**- esta noche**	- esta noche
- one night	**- una noche**	- oona noche
- two nights	**- dos noches**	- dos noches
- a week	**- una semana**	- oona semana
From... (May 1st) to... (May 8th)	**Del... (primero de mayo) al... (ocho de mayo)**	del... (preemero de mayo) al... (ocho de mayo)

Room types

Rooms fall into several standard sizes: king, queen, twin (two beds), matrimonial (one bed) and double-double (four-person). Even the simplest establishments offer a private bathroom with hot water.

Do you have... room?	¿Tiene una habitación...	tyene oona abeeta-syon...
- a single	- sencilla?	- senseeya?
- a double	- doble?	- doble?
- a family	- para una familia?	- para oona fameelya?
with...	con...	kon...
- a cot?	- una cuna?	- oona koona?
- twin beds?	- dos camas twin?	- dos kamas tween?
- a double bed?	- una cama matrimonial?	- oona kama matreemonyal?
- a bath/shower?	- bañera/ducha?	- banyera/doocha?
- air conditioning?	- aire acondicionado?	- ayre akondeesyonado?
- Internet access?	- acceso a internet?	- akseso a eenternet?
Can I see the room?	¿Puedo ver la habitación?	pwedo ber la abeetasyon?

Mexican cowboys

Family-run ranches welcome "dudes" now: city slickers keen to bike, hike or ride horses. These establishments usually whip up terrific, authentic grub.

Price levels

Latin America remains popular among budget travellers, but high-end resorts cater to the ever-larger posh crowd. Low wages translate into extreme luxury on the cheap here: supervillas may have a staff of 16 pampering six guests, for example.

How much is...	¿Cuánto cuesta...	kwanto kwesta...
- a double room?	- una habitación doble?	- oona abeetasyon doble?

English	Spanish	Pronunciation
- per night?	- por noche?	- por <u>no</u>che?
- per week?	- por semana?	- por se<u>ma</u>na?
Is breakfast included?	¿Está incluido el desayuno?	es<u>tah</u> eenkloo<u>ee</u>do el desa<u>yoo</u>no?
Do you have...	¿Tienen...	<u>ty</u>enen...
- a reduction for children?	- descuentos para niños?	- des<u>kwen</u>tos <u>pa</u>ra <u>nee</u>nyos?
- a single room supplement?	- suplemento por habitación sencilla?	- soople<u>men</u>to <u>pa</u>ra abeeta<u>syon</u> sen<u>see</u>ya?
Is there...	¿Hay...	ai...
- a swimming pool?	- piscina?	- pee<u>see</u>na?
- an elevator?	- elevador?	- eleba<u>dor</u>?
I'll take it	La tomo	la <u>to</u>mo
Can I pay by...	¿Puedo pagar con...	<u>pwe</u>do pa<u>gar</u> kon...
- credit card?	- tarjeta de crédito?	- tar<u>het</u>ta de <u>kre</u>deeto?
- traveller's cheques?	- cheques de viajero?	- <u>che</u>kes de beea-<u>he</u>ro?

In the coral garden

The clear, turquoise waters of the Caribbean lure snorkellers and divers. Eager to learn? Most scuba schools can issue a "tropical referral certificate". Students complete the coursework and pool-time at home, then finish the practise dives on holiday.

Special requests

Could you...	¿Podría...	podreea...
- put this in the hotel safe?	- poner esto en la caja de seguridad del hotel?	- poner esto en la kaha de segooreedad del otel?
- order a taxi for me?	- pedirme un taxi?	- pedeerme oon taksee?
- wake me up at (7am)?	- despertarme a las (siete) de la mañana?	- despertarme a las (syete) de la manyana?
Can I have...	Quiero una habitación...	kyero oona abeeta-syon...
- a room with a sea view?	- con vista al mar	- kon beesta al mar
- a bigger room?	- más grande	- mas grande
- a quieter room?	- más tranquila	- mas trankeela
Is there...	¿Hay...	ai...
- a safe?	- caja de seguridad?	- kaha de segooreedad?
- a babysitting service?	- servicio de niñera?	- serbeesyo de neenyera?
- a laundry service?	- servicio de lavandería?	- serbeesyo de labandereea?
Is there wheelchair access?	¿Hay acceso para silla de ruedas?	ai akseso para seeya de rwedas?

Checking in & out

I have a reservation for tonight	Tengo una reserva para esta noche	tengo oona reserba para esta noche
In the name of...	A nombre de...	a nombre de...
Here's my passport	Aquí tiene mi pasaporte	akee tyene mee pasaporte
What time is check out?	¿A qué hora hay que dejar la habitación?	a keh ora ai ke dehar la abeetasyon?
Can I have a later check out?	¿Puedo salir más tarde?	pwedo saleer mas tarde?

47

Can I leave my bags here?	¿Puedo dejar mis maletas aquí?	pwedo dehar mees maletas akee?
I'd like to check out	Quiero marcharme	kyero marcharme
Can I have the bill?	¿Me da la cuenta?	me da la kwenta?

Camping

Do you have...	¿Tienen...	tyenen...
- a site available?	- un espacio libre?	- un espasyo leebre?
- electricity?	- electricidad?	- elektreeseedad?
- hot showers?	- duchas con agua caliente?	- doochas kon agwa kalyente?
- tents for hire?	- tiendas para alquilar?	tyendas para alkeelar?

How much is it per...	¿Cuánto cuesta por...	kwanto kwesta por...
- tent?	- tienda de campaña?	- tyenda de kampanya?
- caravan?	- caravana?	- karabana?
- person?	- persona?	- persona?
- car?	- carro?	- karro?

Where is/are...	¿Dónde está/están...	dondeh estah/estan...
- the reception?	- la recepción?	- la resepsyon?
- the bathrooms?	- los baños?	- los banyos?
- the laundry facilities?	- la lavandería?	- la labandereea?

Education in the jungle

Experienced guides lead visitors through Costa Rica's cloud forests. Butterflies soar through the jungle canopy. Sloths dangle from branches. Perhaps you'll even glimpse a jaguar prowling the mountains.

Survival guide

Major credit cards work in almost every Latin American country... sometimes – and only in certain establishments. ATMs can also be unreliable. Savvy tourists carry local currency, traveller's cheques and back-up cards. Register your itinerary with banks and credit card companies, so the fraud departments don't freeze your accounts.

Plan ahead and be patient: these countries don't enjoy the availability and quality of services – bank, communication and health – as the UK.

Money/banks

Where is the nearest...	¿Dónde está el... más cercano?	_dondeh estah el... mas serkano?_
- bank?	- banco	- _banko_
- ATM/bank machine?	- cajero automático	- _kahero owtomateeko_
Where is the nearest foreign exchange office?	¿Dónde está la casa de cambio más cercana?	- _dondeh estah la kasa de kambyo mas serkana?_
I'd like to...	Quisiera...	_keesyera..._
- withdraw money	- sacar dinero	- _sakar deenero_
- cash a traveller's cheque	- cobrar un cheque de viajero	- _kobrar oon cheke de beeahero_
- change money	- cambiar dinero	- _kambyar deenero_
- arrange a transfer	- hacer una transferencia	- _aser oona transferensya_
What's the exchange rate?	¿A cuánto está el cambio?	_a kwanto estah el kambyo?_

Banks

A visit to the typically bank demands a lot of time and patience. Prepare for red tape and infuriating bureaucracy. A **casa de cambio** changes money more quickly.

What's the commission?	¿Cuánto es la comisión?	_kwanto es la komeesyon?_
What's the charge for...	¿Cuánto es la comisión por...	_kwanto es la komeesyon por..._
- making a withdrawal?	- sacar dinero?	- _sakar deenero?_

- exchanging money?	- **cambiar dinero?**	*- kambyar deenero?*
- cashing a cheque?	- **cobrar un cheque?**	*- kobrar oon cheke?*
This is not right	**Esto no es correcto**	*esto no es korrekto*
Is there a problem with my account?	**¿Hay algún problema con mi cuenta?**	*ai algoon problema kon mee kwenta?*
The ATM/bank machine took my card	**El cajero se ha tragado mi tarjeta**	*el kahero se a tragado mee tarhetta*
I've forgotten my PIN	**Se me ha olvidado mi código PIN**	*se me a olbeedado mi kodeego peen*

Post office

Where is the (main) post office?	**¿Dónde está la oficina (central) de correos?**	*dondeh estah la opheeseena sentral de korreos?*
I'd like to send...	**Quisiera enviar...**	*keesyera enbyar...*
- a letter	- **una carta**	*- oona karta*
- a postcard	- **una postal**	*- oona postal*
- a parcel	- **un paquete**	*- oon pakete*
- a fax	- **un fax**	*- oon phaks*
I'd like to send this...	**Quisiera enviar esto...**	*keesyera enbyar esto...*
- to the United Kingdom	- **al Reino Unido**	*- al reyno ooneedo*
- by airmail	- **por correo aéreo**	*- por korreo aereo*
- by express mail	- **por correo urgente**	*- por korreo oorhente*
- by registered mail	- **por correo certificado**	*- por korreo serteefeekado*
I'd like...	**Quisiera...**	*keesyera...*
- a stamp for this letter/postcard	- **un sello para esta carta/postal**	*- oon seyo para esta karta/postal*
- to buy envelopes	- **comprar sobres**	*- komprar sobres*
- to make a photocopy	- **hacer una fotocopia**	*- aser oona photokopya*

| It contains...
It's fragile | **Contiene...**
Es frágil | *kontyene...*
es phraheel |

Telecoms

Where can I make an international phone call?	**¿Dónde puedo hacer una llamada internacional?**	*dondeh pwedo aser oona yamada eenternasyonal?*
Where can I buy a phone card?	**¿Dónde puedo comprar una tarjeta de teléfono?**	*dondeh pwedo komprar oona tarhetta de telephono?*
How do I call abroad?	**¿Cómo llamo al extranjero?**	*komo yamo al estranhero?*
How much does it cost per minute?	**¿Cuánto cuesta por minuto?**	*kwanto kwesta por meenooto?*
The number is ...	**El número es...**	*el noomero es...*
What's the area/country code for...?	**¿Cuál es el prefijo de la región/del país para...?**	*kwal es el prepheeho de la rehyon/del pays para...?*
The number is engaged	**Está comunicando**	*estah komooneekando*
The connection is bad	**No se oye bien**	*no se oye byen*
I've been cut off	**Se ha cortado**	*se a kortado*
I'd like...	**Quisiera...**	*keesyera...*
- a charger for my mobile phone	**- un cargador para el celular**	*- oon kargador para el seloolar*
- an adaptor plug	**- un adaptador**	*- oon adaptador*
- a pre-paid SIM card	**- una tarjeta SIM de prepago**	*- oona tarhetta seem de prepago*

Internet

Where's the nearest Internet café?	**¿Hay un internet café cerca de aquí?**	*ai oon eenternet kafeh serka de akee?*
Can I access the Internet here?	**¿Tienen acceso a internet?**	*tyenen akseso a eenternet?*
I'd like to...	**Quisiera...**	*keesyera...*
- use the Internet	**- usar internet**	*- oosar eenternet*

- check my email	- **leer mis emails/correos electrónicos**	- _ler mees ee<u>meyls</u>/kor<u>reos</u> elek<u>tro</u>neekos_
- use a printer	- **usar la impresora**	- _oo<u>sar</u> la eempre<u>so</u>ra_
How much is it...	**¿Cuánto cuesta...**	_<u>kwan</u>to <u>kwes</u>ta..._
- per minute?	- **por minuto?**	- _por mee<u>noo</u>to?_
- per hour?	- **por hora?**	- _por <u>o</u>ra?_
- to buy a CD?	- **comprar un CD?**	- _kom<u>prar</u> oon se<u>deh</u>?_
How do I...	**¿Cómo...**	_<u>ko</u>mo.._
- log on?	- **entro al sistema?**	- _<u>en</u>tro al sees<u>te</u>ma?_
- open a browser?	- **abro el navegador?**	- _<u>a</u>bro el nabega<u>dor</u>?_
- print this?	- **imprimo esto?**	- _eem<u>pree</u>mo <u>es</u>to?_
I need help with this computer	**Necesito ayuda con esta computadora**	_nese<u>see</u>to a<u>yoo</u>da kon <u>es</u>ta kompoota<u>do</u>ra_
The computer has crashed	**Se ha colgado la computadora**	_se a kol<u>ga</u>do la kompoota<u>do</u>ra_
I've finished	**He terminado**	_e termee<u>na</u>do_

Internet cafés

In most countries, Internet cafés are common, though only in bigger cities. Connections are slow – Stone Age dial-up slow – so don't attempt anything ambitious. Send larger files through the post on CD instead.

Chemist

Where's the nearest (all-night) pharmacy?	**¿Hay una farmacia de guardia cerca?**	_ai <u>oo</u>na phar<u>ma</u>sya de <u>gwar</u>deea <u>ser</u>ka?_

At what time does the pharmacy open/close?	¿A qué hora abre/cierra la farmacia?	a keh ora abre/syerra la pharmasya?
I need something for...	Necesito algo para...	neseseeto algo para...
- diarrhoea	- la diarrea	- la dyarea
- a cold	- el resfriado	- el resphryado
- a cough	- la tos	- la tos
- insect bites	- las picaduras de insecto	- las peekadooras de eensekto
- sunburn	- las quemaduras de sol	- las kemadooras de sol
- motion sickness	- el mareo	- el mareo
- hay fever	- la alergia al polen	- la alerhya al polen
- period pain	- el dolor de regla	- el dolor de regla
- abdominal pains	- el dolor abdominal	- el dolor abdomeenal
- a urine infection	- la infección urinaria	- la eenpheksyon ooreenaria
I'd like...	Quisiera...	keesyera...
- aspirin	- aspirinas	- apeereenas
- plasters	- curitas	- kooreetas
- condoms	- condones	- kondones
- insect repellent	- repelente de insectos	- repelente de eensektos
- painkillers	- calmantes	- kalmantes
- a contraceptive	- un anticonceptivo	- oon anteekonsepteebo
How much should I take?	¿Cuánto tomo?	kwanto tomo?
Take...	Tome...	tome...
- a tablet	- una pastilla	- oona pasteeya
- a teaspoon	- una cucharadita	- oona koocharadeeta
- with water	- con agua	- kon agwa
How often should I take this?	¿Cuántas veces lo tomo?	kwantas beses lo tomo?
- once/twice a day	- una vez/dos veces al día	- oona bes/dos beses al deea

| - before/after meals | - **antes/después de las comidas** | *- antes/despwes de las komeedas?* |
| - in the morning/ evening | - **por la mañana/ por la noche** | *- por la manyana/ por la noche* |

Is it suitable for children?	**¿Lo pueden tomar los niños?**	*lo pweden tomar los neenyos?*
Will it make me drowsy?	**¿Me va a dar sueño?**	*me ba a dar swenyo?*
Do I need a prescription?	**¿Es con receta?**	*es kon reseta?*
I have a prescription	**Tengo una receta**	*tengo oona reseta*

Children

| Where should I take the children? | **¿Dónde llevo a los niños?** | *dondeh yebo a los neenyos?* |

Where is the nearest...	**¿Hay... cerca?**	*ai... serka?*
- playground?	- **una zona de juegos**	*- oona sona de hwegos*
- fairground?	- **un parque de atracciones**	*- oon parke de atraksyones*
- zoo?	- **un zoo**	*- oon thoh*
- swimming pool?	- **una piscina**	*- oona peeseena*
- park?	- **un parque**	*- oon parke*

Is this suitable for children?	**¿Es apropiado para niños?**	*es apropyado para neenyos?*
Are children allowed?	**¿Pueden entrar niños?**	*pweden entrar neenyos?*
Are there baby-changing facilities here?	**¿Hay cambiadores para bebés aquí?**	*ai kambyadores para bebes akee?*

Do you have...	**¿Tienen...**	*tyenen...*
- a children's menu?	- **menú infantil?**	*- menoo een-phanteel?*
- a high chair?	- **tronas para bebés?**	*- tronas para bebes?*

| Is there... | **¿Hay...** | *ai..* |
| - a child-minding service? | - **niñeras/nanas?** | *- neenyeras/nanas?* |

55

- a nursery?	- guardería infantil?	- gwarderya een-phanteel?
Can you recommend a reliable babysitter?	¿Me puede recomendar una niñera de confianza?	me pwede rekomendar oona neenyera de konpheeansa?
What time do I have to pick them up?	¿A qué hora los recojo?	a keh ora los reko-ho?
He/she is... years old	El/ella tiene... años	El/eya tyeneh... anyos
I'd like to buy...	Quisiera comprar...	keesyera komprar...
- nappies	- pañales	- panyales
- baby wipes	- toallitas húmedas para bebés	- toayeetas oomedas para bebes
- tissues	- pañuelos	- panwelos

Travellers with disabilities

I have a disability	Soy discapacitado	soy deeskapaseetado
I need assistance	Necesito ayuda	neseseeto ayooda
I am blind	Soy ciego/a	soy syego/a
I am deaf	Soy sordo/a	soy sordo/a
I have a hearing aid	Llevo un aparato para sordos	yebo oon aparato para sordos
I can't walk well	No camino bien	no cameeno byen
Is there a lift?	¿Hay ascensor?	ai asensor?
Is there wheelchair access?	¿Hay acceso para sillas de ruedas?	ai akseso para seeyas de rwedas?
Can I bring my guide dog?	¿Puedo traer a mi perro guía?	pwedo traer a mee perro gya?
Are there disabled toilets?	¿Hay sanitarios para discapacitados?	ai saneetaryos para deeskapaseetados?
Do you offer disabled services?	¿Tienen servicios para discapacitados?	tyenen serbeesyos para deeskapaseetados?
Could you help me...	¿Me puede ayudar a...	me pwede ayoodar a...

- cross the street?	- cruzar la calle?	- kroo*sar* la *kaye*?
- go up/down the stairs?	- subir/bajar las escaleras?	- soo*beer*/ba*har* las eska*leras*?
Can I sit down somewhere?	¿Me puedo sentar en algún sitio?	me *pwedo* sen*tar* en al*goon* *seetyo*?
Could you call a disabled taxi for me?	¿Puede llamar un taxi para discapacitados?	*pwede* ya*mar* oon *taksee* *para* deeskapasee*tados*?

Repairs & cleaning

This is broken	Esto está roto	*esto* es*tah* *roto*
Can you fix it?	¿Puede arreglarlo?	*pwede* arre*glar*lo?
Do you have...	¿Tiene...	*tyene*...
- a battery?	- una batería?	- *oona* bate*reea*?
- spare parts?	- piezas de recambio?	- *pyesas* de re*kam*byo?
Can you...this?	¿Puede...esto?	*pwede*...*esto*?
- clean	- limpiar	- leem*pyar*
- press	- planchar	- plan*char*
- dry-clean	- lavar en seco	- la*var* en *seko*
- patch	- arreglar	arre*glar*
When will it be ready?	¿Cuándo estará listo?	*kwando* esta*rah* *leesto*?
This isn't mine	Esto no es mío	*esto* no es *meeo*

Tourist information

Where's the Tourist Information Office?	¿Dónde está la oficina de turismo?	*dondeh* es*tah* la ophee*seena* de too*reesmo*?

Tourist information

Popular destinations have tourist offices with brochures and English-speaking personnel.
The same cannot be said for areas off the beaten path, however.

Do you have a city/regional map?	¿Tiene un plano de la ciudad/región?	tyene oon plano de la syoodad/rehyon?
What are the main places of interest?	¿Cuáles son los principales lugares de interés?	kwales son los preenseepales loogares de eenteres?
Could you show me on the map?	¿Me puede indicar dónde está en el plano?	me pwede eendeekar dondeh estah en el plano?
We'll be here for...	Estaremos aquí por...	estaremos akee por...
- half a day	- medio día	- medyo deea
- a day	- un día	- oon deea
- a week	- una semana	- oona semana
Do you have a brochure in English?	¿Tiene un folleto en inglés?	tyene oon phoyeto en eengles?
We're interested in...	Nos interesa...	nos eenteresa...
- history	- la historia	- la eestorya
- architecture	- la arquitectura	- la arkeetektoora
- shopping	- ir de compras	- eer de kompras
- hiking	- andar por el monte	- andar por el monte
- a scenic walk	- un paseo	- oon paseo
- a boat cruise	- un viaje en barco	- oon byahe en barko
- a guided tour	- una visita guiada	- oona beeseeta gyada
Are there any excursions?	¿Hay alguna excursión?	ai algoona ekskoorsyon?
How long does it take?	¿Cuánto dura?	kwanto doora?
Are there any tours in English?	¿Hay alguna visita en inglés?	ai algoona beeseeta en eengles?

Emergencies

Latin America has a reputation for
sensational landscapes, colonial cities,
pre-Colombian sites, and, well, danger.
However, most annoyances can be
avoided: prepare well and respect certain
rules. Street crime is the highest threat.
Dress down and leave the diamonds back
home. Lock all valuables into a safe and
carry a photocopy of your passport. Be
alert for pickpockets on public transport
and avoid bogus taxis (cab stands are
more reliable). Health-wise, get all
necessary vaccinations, bring efficient
insect repellent and don't eat snacks from
street stands.

Medical

Where is the...	¿Dónde está el...	*dondeh estah el...*
- hospital?	- hospital?	*- ospeetal?*
- health centre?	- ambulatorio?	*- amboolatoryo?*

I need...	Necesito...	*neseseeto...*
- a doctor	- un médico	*- oon medeeko*
- a female doctor	- una doctora	*- oona doktora*
- an ambulance	- una ambulancia	*- oona amboolansya*
It´s very urgent	Es muy urgente	*es mooy oorhente*
I´m injured	Estoy herido/a	*estoy ereedo/a*

Can I see the doctor?	¿Puedo ver al médico?	*pwedo ber al medeeko?*
I don´t feel well	No me siento bien	*no me syento byen*
I have...	Tengo...	*tengo...*
- a cold	- resfriado	*- resphryado*
- diarrhoea	- diarrea	*- deearrea*
- a rash	- un sarpullido	*- oon sarpooyeedo*
- a temperature	- fiebre	*- phyebre*
I have a lump here	Tengo un hinchazón aquí	*tengo oon eenchason akee*
Can I have the morning-after pill?	¿Me da la píldora del día después?	*me da la peeldora del deea despwes?*

It hurts here	Me duele aquí	*me dwele akee*
It hurts a lot / a little	Me duele mucho/poco	*me dwele moocho/poko*

Portable pharmacy
Don't leave home without a comprehensive first aid kit. Some standards include bandages, antiseptic cream, aspirin, scissors, sunscreen, diarrhoea medication, stomach-calming tablets. Ensure medication is clearly labelled and even accompanied by a letter from your GP, to avoid problems at customs.

How much do I owe you?	**¿Cuánto le debo?**	*kwanto le debo?*
I have insurance	**Tengo seguro**	*tengo segooro*

Dentist

I need a dentist	**Necesito ver a un dentista**	*neseseeto ber a oon denteesta*
I have tooth ache	**Tengo dolor de muelas**	*tengo dolor de mooelas*
My gums are swollen	**Tengo las encías inflamadas**	*tengo las enseeas eenphlamadas*
This filling has fallen out	**Se me ha caído este empaste**	*se me a kaeedo este empaste*
I have an abscess	**Tengo un flemón**	*tengo oon phlemon*
I´ve broken a tooth	**Me he roto un diente**	*me e rotto oon dyente*
Are you going to take it out?	**¿Me lo/la va a sacar?**	*me lo/la ba a sakar?*
Can you fix it temporarily?	**¿Lo puede arreglar provisionalmente?**	*lo pwede arreglar probeesyonalmente?*

Crime

I want to report a theft	**Quiero denunciar un robo**	*kyero denoonsyar oon robo*
Someone has stolen my...	**Me han robado...**	*me an robado*
- bag	**- la bolsa**	*- la bolsa*
- car	**- el carro**	*- el karro*
- credit cards	**- las tarjetas de crédito**	*- las tarhettas de kredeeto*
- money	**- el dinero**	*- el deenero*
- passport	**- el pasaporte**	*- el pasaporte*
I´ve been attacked	**Me han agredido**	*me an agredeedo*

Lost property

I´ve lost my...	**He perdido...**	*e perdeedo...*
- car keys	**- las llaves del carro**	*- las yabes del karro*
- driving licence	**- la licencia de manejar**	*- la leesensya de manehar*
- handbag	**- el bolso**	*- el bolso*
- flight tickets	**- los boletos de avión**	*- los boletos de abyon*

61

It happened...	**Ocurrió...**	*okoorryo...*
- this morning	**- esta mañana**	*- esta manyana*
- today	**- hoy**	*- oy*
- in the hotel	**- en el hotel**	*- en el otel*
I left it in the taxi	**Lo/a dejé en el taxi**	*lo/a deheh en el tak-see*

Breakdowns

I´ve had...	**He tenido...**	*e teneedo...*
- an accident	**- un accidente**	*- oon akseedente*
- a breakdown	**- una avería**	*- oona abereea*
- a puncture	**- un pinchazo**	*- oon peenchaso*

My battery is flat	**No tengo batería**	*no tengo batereea*
I don´t have a spare tyre	**No tengo rueda de repuesto**	*no tengo rweda de repwesto*
I´ve run out of petrol	**Me he quedado sin gasolina**	*me e kedado seen gasoleena*
My car doesn´t start	**No me arranca el carro**	*no me arranka el karro*

Can you repair it?	**¿Puede arreglarlo?**	*pwede arreglarlo?*
How long will you be?	**¿Cuánto va a tardar?**	*kwanto ba a tardar?*
I have breakdown cover	**Tengo seguro de asistencia en carretera**	*tengo segooro de aseestensya en karretera*

Problems with the authorities

I´m sorry, I didn´t realise...	**Lo siento, no me dí cuenta de que...**	*lo syento, no me dee kwenta de ke...*
- I was driving so fast	**- conducía tan rápido**	*- kondooseea tan rapeedo*
- I went over the red lights	**- crucé con el semáforo en rojo**	*- krooseh kon el semaphoro en roho*
- it was against the law	**- eso era ilegal**	*- eso era eelegal*

| Here are my documents | **Aquí tiene mis documentos** | *akee tyene mees dokoomentos* |
| I´m innocent | **Soy inocente** | *soy eenosente* |

40. ¡Qué cosa tan curiosa! La torre de
    A. estuviera   B. está caída
       cayéndose

41. No me parece que esto ... una uto
    A. estaría   B. era

42. Roberto, estoy sin un cobre. Ter
    ¿A quién ... venderás?
    A. se   B. te lo

43. Disculpa Marcos, la solución o
    A. al/adecuada   B. a el/c

44. ¿Me puedes explicar
    A. niegas

Dictionary

This section consists of two parts: an
English-Latin American Spanish
dictionary to help you get your point
across and a Latin American Spanish-
English one to decipher the reply. In
the Spanish, we list nouns with their
article: **el** for masculine, **la** for
feminine and **los** or **las** for plural.
If nouns can be either masculine or
feminine, we display both: **el/la niño/a**
(child) means **el niño** is a male child
(i.e. a boy), **la niña** the female version
(a girl). For adjectives we do the same:
"-o" is the masculine form (**niño
cansado** – tired boy), "-a" the feminine
(**niña cansada** – tired girl).

English-Latin American Spanish dictionary

A

English	Spanish	Pronunciation
a (n)	un/a	oon/a
about (concerning)	sobre	sobre
accident	el accidente	el akseedente
accommodation	el alojamiento	el alohamyento
A&E	urgencias	oorhenseeas
aeroplane	el avión	el abyon
again	otra vez	otra bes
ago	hace	ase
AIDS	el SIDA	el seeda
airmail	el correo aéreo	el korreo aereo

airport	el aeropuerto	el aeropooerto

Latin America's most modern hub is Santiago de Querétaro, Mexico.

English	Spanish	Pronunciation
alarm	la alarma	la alarma
all	todo/a (s)	todo/a (s)
all right	de acuerdo	de akwerdo
allergy	la alergia	la alerhya
ambulance	la ambulancia	la ambolansya
America	América	amereeka
American	americano/a	amereekano/a
and	y	ee
anniversary	el aniversario	el aneebersaryo
another	otro/a (s)	otro/a (s)
to answer	responder	responder
any	alguno/a (s)/ninguno/a (s)	algoono/a (s)/ningoono/a (s)
apartment	el apartamento	el apartamento
appointment	la cita	la seeta
April	abril	abreel
area	el área	el areya
area code	el prefijo	el prepheeho
around	alrededor (de)	alrededor (de)
to arrange	organizar	organeesar
arrival	la llegada	la yegada
art	el arte	el arte
to ask	preguntar	pregoontar
aspirin	la aspirina	la aspeereena
at	en	en
August	agosto	agosto
Australia	Australia	awstralya
Australian	australiano/a	awstralyano/a
available	disponible	deesponeeble
away	lejos	lehos

B

baby	el bebé	el be*beh*
back (body)	espalda	es*palda*
back (place)	atrás	*atras*
baggage	el equipaje	el ekee*pahe*
bar (pub)	el bar	el bar
bath	el baño	el *banyo*
bathing cap	el gorro de baño	el *gorro* de *banyo*
to be	ser/estar	ser/es*tar*

beach **la playa** *la playa*
Watch out for sand fleas on those gorgeous tropical playas.
Vitamin B prevents the bites from welting sometimes.

because	porque	*porkeh*
best	el/la/lo mejor	el/la/lo me*hor*
better	mejor	me*hor*
between	entre	*entre*
bicycle	la bicicleta	la beesee*kletta*
big	grande	*grande*
bill	la cuenta	la *kwenta*
bit (a)	un poco	un *poko*
boarding card	la tarjeta de embarque	la tar*hetta* de em*barke*
book	el libro	el *leebro*
to book	reservar	reser*bar*
booking	la reserva	la re*serba*
box office	la taquilla	la ta*keeya*
boy	el chico	el *cheeko*
brother	el hermano	el er*mano*
bullfight	la corrida de toros	la ko*rreeda* de *torros*
bureau de change	la casa de cambio	la *kasa* de *kamb*yo
to burn	quemar	ke*mar*
bus	el autobús	el awto*boos*
business	el negocio	el ne*gosyo*
business class	la clase preferente	la *klase* prephe*rente*
but	pero	*pero*
to buy	comprar	kom*prar*
by (beside)	al lado (de)	al *lado* (de)
by (by air, car)	en (en avión, en carro)	en (en a*byon*, en *karro*)
by (via)	por	por

C

café	la cafetería	la kaphete*reea*
calculator	la calculadora	la kalkoola*dora*
to call	llamar	ya*mar*
camera	la cámara fotográfica	la *kamara* pho-togra*pheeka*
can (to be able)	poder	po*der*
to cancel	cancelar	kanse*lar*
car	el carro	el *karro*
carton (cigarettes)	el cartón	el kar*ton*
cash	el dinero en efectivo	el dee*nero* en ephek*teebo*

cash point	el cajero automático	el *kahero awtomateeko*
casino	el casino	el *kaseeno*
cathedral	la catedral	la *katedral*
cd	el cd	el *sedeh*
centre	el centro	el *sentro*
to change	cambiar	*kambyar*
charge	el precio	el *presyo*
to charge	cobrar	*kobrar*
cheap	barato/a	*barato/a*
to check in (airport)	facturar	*phaktoorar*
to check in (hotel)	registrarse	*reheestrarse*
cheque	el cheque	el *cheke*
child	el/la niño/a	el/la *neenyo/a*
cigar	el puro	el *pooro*
cigarette	el cigarrillo	el *seegareeyo*
cinema	el cine	el *seene*
city	la ciudad	la *seeoodad*
to close	cerrar	*serrar*
close by	cerca de	*serka de*
closed	cerrado/a	*serrado/a*
clothes	la ropa	la *ropa*
club	el club	el *kloob*
coast	la costa	la *kosta*
cold	frío/a	*phreeo/a*

colour	**el color**	*el kolor*

The hand-woven textiles of the Mayans' descendants contain a stunning array of tones.

to complain	reclamar	*reklamar*
complaint	la reclamación	la *reklamasyon*
computer	la computadora	la *kompootadora*
to confirm	confirmar	*konpheermar*
confirmation	la confirmación	la *konpheermasyon*
congratulations!	¡felicidades!	*feleeseedades!*
consulate	el consulado	el *konsoolado*
to contact	ponerse en contacto	*ponerse en kontakto*
contagious	contagioso/a	*kontahyoso/a*
cool	fresco/a	*phresko/a*
cost	el precio	el *presyo*
to cost	costar	*kostar*
cot	la cuna	la *koona*
country	el país	el *pays*
countryside	el campo	el *kampo*
cream	la crema	la *krema*
credit card	la tarjeta de crédito	la *tarhetta de kredeeto*
crime	el delito	el *deleeto*
currency	la moneda	la *moneda*
customer	el cliente	el *klyente*
customs	la aduana	la *adooana*
cut	el corte	el *korte*
to cut	cortar	*kortar*
cycling	el ciclismo	el *seekleesmo*

D

damage	el/los daño/s	el/los danyos
date (calendar)	la fecha	la phecha
daughter	la hija	la eeha
day	el día	el deea

December   **diciembre**   *deesyembre*
Celebrate Chistmas on a Central American beach, helping to protect nesting sea turtles.

to dehydrate	deshidratar	deseedratar
delay	el retraso	el retraso
to dial	marcar	markar
difficult	difícil	deepheesyl
dining room	el comedor	el komedor
directions	las instrucciones	las eenstrooksyones
dirty	sucio/a	soosyo/a
disable	discapacitado/a	deeskapaseetado/a
disco	la discoteca	la deeskoteka
discount	el descuento	el deskwento
disinfectant	el desinfectante	el deseenphektante
to disturb	molestar	molestar
doctor	el/la médico/a	el/la medeeko/a
double	doble	doble
down	abajo	abaho
to drive	manejar	manehar
driver	el/la conductor/a/ el/la chofer	el/la kondooktora/ el/la chopher
driving licence	la licencia de manejar	la leesensya de manehar
drug	la medicina	la medeeseena
to dry-clean	lavar en seco	labar en sekko
dry-cleaner's	la tintorería	la teentorereea
during	durante	doorante
duty (tax)	los impuestos	los eempooestos

E

early	temprano	temprano
to eat	comer	komer
e-mail	el email/el correo electrónico	el eemeyl/el korreo elektroneeko
embassy	la embajada	la embahada
emergency	la emergencia	la emerhensya
England	Inglaterra	eenglaterra
English	inglés/esa	eengles/esa
to enjoy	divertirse	deeberteerse
enough	bastante	bastante
error	el error	el error
exactly	exactamente	eksaktamente
exchange rate	el cambio	el kambeeo
exhibition	la exposición	la eksposeesyon
to export	exportar	eksportar
express (delivery)	urgente	oorhente
express (train)	rápido	rapeedo

F

| facilities | las instalaciones | *las eenstalasyones* |
| far | lejos | *lehos* |

fast	rápido	*rapeedo*
Traffic blasts along at a pace many visitors find **muy rápido**. Weigh the options carefully before renting a car.		

father	el padre	*el padre*
favourite	favorito/a	*faboreeto/a*
to fax	mandar por fax	*mandar por phaks*
filling (station)	la gasolinera	*la gasoleenera*
February	febrero	*febrero*
film (camera)	el rollo	*el royo*
film (cinema)	la película	*la peleecoola*
to finish	terminar	*termeenar*
fire	el fuego	*el phooego*
first aid	los primeros auxilios	*los preemeros awkseelyos*
fitting room	el probador	*el probador*
flight	el vuelo	*el booelo*
flu	la gripe	*la greepe*
food poisoning	la intoxicación alimenticia	*la eentokseekasyon aleementeesya*
football	el fútbol	*el phootbol*
for	por/para	*por/para*
form (document)	el impreso	*el eempreso*
free (money)	gratis	*gratees*
free (vacant)	libre	*leebre*
friend	amigo/a	*ameego/a*
from	de/desde	*de/desde*

G

gallery	la galería	*la galereea*
garage	el garage	*el garahe*
gas	el gas	*el gas*
gents	los sanitarios de caballeros	*los saneetaryos de kabayeros*
to get	obtener	*obtener*
girl	la chica	*la cheeka*
to give	dar	*dar*
glasses	las lentes/los anteojos	*las lentes/los anteohos*
to go	ir	*eer*
golf	el golf	*el golph*
golf course	el campo de golf	*el kampo de golf*
good	bueno/a	*bweno/a*
group	el grupo	*el groopo*
guarantee	la garantía	*la garanteea*
guide	la guía	*la geea*

H

| hair | el pelo | *el pelo* |

hairdresser's	la peluquería	la pelookereea
half	medio/a	medeeo/a
to have	tener	tener
heat	el calor	el kalor
help!	¡socorro!	sokorro!
to help	ayudar	ayoodar
here	aquí	akee
high	alto/a	alto/a

hire **aliquilar** *alkeelar*
Timid drivers – and those tired of public transport –
should hire a taxi for a whole day.

holiday	la fiesta	la fyesta
holidays	las vacaciones	las bakasyones
homosexual	homosexual	omoseksooal
horse riding	montar a caballo	montar a kabayo
hospital	el hospital	el ospeetal
hot	caliente	kalyente
how?	¿cómo?	komo
how big?	¿de qué tamaño?	de keh tamanyo?
how far?	¿a qué distancia?	a keh deestansya?
how long?	¿cuánto tiempo?	kwanto tyempo?

How much? **¿cuánto?** *kwanto?*
Haggling in markets is the norm. Turn around, pretend
to leave and the price plummets.

to be hungry	tener hambre	tener ambre
hurry up!	¡de prisa!	de preesa!
to hurt	doler	doler
husband	el marido	el mareedo

I

identity card	el carnet de identidad	el karneh de eedenteedad
ill	enfermo/a	enfermo/a
immediately	inmediatamente	eemedyatamente
to import	importar	eemportar
important	importante	eemportante
in	en	en
information	la información	la eenphormasyon
inside	dentro (de)	dentro (de)
insurance	el seguro	el segooro
interesting	interesante	eenteresante
international	internacional	eenternasyonal
Ireland	Irlanda	eerlanda
Irish	irlandés/esa	eerlandes/esa
island	la isla	la eesla
itinerary	el itinerario	el eeteeneraryo

J

English	Spanish	Pronunciation
January	**enero**	*enero*
jellyfish	**la medusa**	*la medoosa*
jet ski	**la moto acuática**	*la moto akwateeka*
journey	**el viaje**	*el byahe*
junction	**el cruce**	*el kroose*
June	**junio**	*hoonyo*
July	**julio**	*hoolyo*
just (only)	**sólo**	*solo*

K

English	Spanish	Pronunciation
to keep	**guardar**	*gwardar*
key	**la llave**	*la yabe*
key ring	**el llavero**	*el yabero*
keyboard	**el teclado**	*el teklado*
kid	**el/la niño/a**	*el/la neenyo/a*
to kill	**matar**	*matar*
kind (nice)	**amable**	*amable*
kind (sort)	**la clase**	*la klase*
kiosk	**el quiosco**	*el kyosko*
kiss	**el beso**	*el beso*
to kiss	**besar**	*besar*
to knock	**golpear**	*golpear*
to know (knowledge)	**saber**	*saber*
to know (person)	**conocer**	*konoser*

L

English	Spanish	Pronunciation
label	**la etiqueta**	*la eteeketta*
ladies (toilets)	**los sanitarios de señoras**	*los saneetaryos de senyoras*
lady	**la señora**	*la senyora*
language	**el idioma**	*el eedeeoma*
last	**el/la último/a**	*el/la oolteemo/a*
late (delayed)	**tarde**	*tarde*

---

late (time)	**retrasado/a**	*retrasado/a*

Latin Americans' sense of time is quite fluid. Studies show that 12 minutes is "late" in the UK. Here the clock might spin two or three hours before someone is "**tarde**".

English	Spanish	Pronunciation
launderette	**la lavandería**	*la labandereea*
lawyer	**el/la abogado**	*el/la abogado*
to leave	**salir**	*saleer*
left	**la izquierda**	*la eeskyerda*
less	**menos**	*menos*
letter	**la carta**	*la karta*
library	**la biblioteca**	*la beeblyoteka*
life jacket	**el chaleco salvavidas**	*el chaleco salbabeedas*
lifeguard	**el/la socorrista**	*el/la sokorreesta*
lift	**el elevador**	*el elebador*
to like	**gustar**	*goostar*
to listen to	**escuchar**	*eskoochar*
little (a little)	**un poco**	*oon poko*

local	**local**	*lokal*
to look	**mirar**	*meerar*
to lose	**perder**	*perder*
lost property	**los objetos perdidos**	*los obhetos perdeedos*
luggage	**el equipaje**	*el ekeepahe*

M

madam	**la señora**	*la senyora*
mail	**el correo**	*el korreo*
main	**principal**	*preenseepal*
to make	**hacer**	*aser*
man	**el hombre**	*el ombre*
manager	**el/la director/a**	*el/la deerektor/a*
many	**muchos/as**	*moochos/as*
map (city)	**el plano**	*el plano*
map (road)	**el mapa**	*el mapa*
March	**marzo**	*marso*

| market | **mercado** | *el merkado* |

Explore local art and crafts in a **mercado de artesanía**.

married	**casado/a**	*kasado/a*
May	**mayo**	*mayo*
maybe	**quizás**	*keesas*
mechanic	**el/la mecánico/a**	*el/la mekaneeko/a*
to meet	**encontrar**	*enkontrar*
meeting	**la reunión**	*la reoonyon*
message	**el recado**	*el rekado*
midday	**el mediodía**	*el medyodeea*
midnight	**la medianoche**	*la medyanoche*
minimum	**mínimo/a**	*meeneemo/a*
minute	**el minuto**	*el meenooto*
to miss (a person)	**echar de menos**	*echar de menos*
to miss (a train)	**perder**	*perder*
missing	**desaparecido/a**	*desapareseedo/a*
mobile phone	**el (teléfono) celular**	*el (telephono) seloolar*
moment	**el momento**	*el momento*
money	**el dinero**	*el deenero*
more	**más**	*mas*
mosquito	**el mosquito**	*el moskeeto*
most	**la mayoría**	*la mayoreea*
mother	**la madre**	*la madre*
much	**mucho**	*moocho*
museum	**el museo**	*el mooseo*
musical	**el musical**	*el mooseekal*
must	**tener que**	*tener ke*
my	**mi**	*mee*

N

name	**el nombre**	*el nombre*
nationality	**la nacionalidad**	*la nasyonalidad*
near	**cerca (de)**	*serka (de)*
necessary	**necesario/a**	*nesesaryo/a*

to need	necesitar	*neseseetar*
never	nunca	*noonka*
new	nuevo/a	*nwebo/a*
news	las noticias	*las noteesyas*
newspaper	el periódico	*el peryodeeko*
next	el/la siguiente	*el/la seegyente*
next to	al lado de	*al lado de*
nice (people)	simpático/a	*seempateeko/a*
nice (things)	bonito/a	*boneeto/a*
night	la noche	*la noche*
nightclub	la sala de fiestas	*la sala de fyestas*
north	el norte	*el norte*
note (money)	el billete	*el beeyete*
nothing	nada	*nada*

| November | noviembre | *nobyembre* |

The **Día de Muertos** (Day of the Dead) in November is Mexico's most impressive **fiesta**.

now	ahora	*aora*
nowhere	en ningún sitio	*en neengoon seeteeo*
nudist beach	la playa nudista	*la playa noodeesta*
number	el número	*el noomero*

O

object	el objeto	*el obheto*
October	octubre	*oktoobre*
off (food)	malo/a	*malo/a*
off (switched)	apagado/a	*apagado/a*
office	la oficina	*la opheeseena*
ok	de acuerdo	*de akwerdo*
on	en	*en*
once	una vez	*oona bes*
only	sólo	*solo*
open	abierto/a	*abyerto/a*
to open	abrir	*abreer*
operator	el/la telefonista	*el/la telephoneesta*
opposite (place)	enfrente (de)	*enphrente (de)*
optician's	la óptica	*la opteeka*
or	o	*o*
to order	pedir	*pedeer*
other	otro/a	*otro/a*
out of order	estropeado/a	*estropeado/a*
outdoor	al aire libre	*al ayre leebre*
outside	fuera (de)	*phwera (de)*
overnight	por la noche	*por la noche*
owner	el/la dueño/a	*el/la dwenyo/a*
oxygen	el oxígeno	*el okseeheno*

P

painkiller	el calmante	*el kalmante*
pair	el par	*el par*
parents	los padres	*los padres*

park	**el parque**	*el parke*
to park	**aparcar**	*aparkar*
parking	**el estacionamiento**	*el estasyonamyento*
party	**la fiesta**	*le fyesta*
passport	**el pasaporte**	*el pasaporte*
to pay	**pagar**	*pagar*
people	**la gente**	*la hente*
perhaps	**quizás**	*keesas*
person	**la persona**	*la persona*
phone	**el teléfono**	*el telephono*
to phone	**llamar por teléfono**	*yamar por telephono*
photo	**la foto**	*la photo*
phrase book	**la guía de conversación**	*la geea de konbersasyon*
place	**el lugar**	*el loogar*
platform	**el andén**	*el anden*
police	**la policía**	*la poleeseea*
port (sea)	**el puerto**	*el pwerto*
possible	**posible**	*poseeble*
post	**el correo**	*el korreo*
post office	**la oficina de correos**	*la opheeseena de korreos*
to prefer	**preferir**	*prefeereer*
prescription	**la receta**	*la reseta*
pretty	**bonito/a**	*boneeto/a*
price	**el precio**	*el presyo*
private	**privado/a**	*preebado/a*
probably	**probablemente**	*probablemente*
problem	**el problema**	*el problema*
pub	**el bar**	*el bar*
public transport	**el transporte público**	*el transporte poobleeko*
to put	**poner**	*poner*

Q

quality	**la calidad**	*la kaleedad*
quantity	**la cantidad**	*la kanteedad*
quarter	**el cuarto**	*el kwarto*
query	**la pregunta**	*la pregoonta*
question	**la pregunta**	*la pregoonta*
queue	**la cola**	*la cola*
quick	**rápido/a**	*rapeedo/a*
quickly	**de prisa**	*de preesa*

| quiet | **tranquilo/a** | *trankeelo/a* |

Latin American cities are anything but quiet: crowded, chaotic and loud. Head into the hills or towards a remote beach for less noise.

| quite | **bastante** | *bastante* |

R

| radio | **la radio** | *la radyo* |
| railway | **el ferrocarril** | *el pherrokarryl* |

rain	la lluvia	la _yoob_ya
rape	la violación	la beeola_syon_
razor blade	la hoja de afeitar	la _o_ha de apha_ytar_
ready	listo/a	_lees_to/a
real	real	re_al_
receipt	el recibo	el re_seebo_
to receive	recibir	resee_beer_
reception	la recepción	la resep_syon_
receptionist	el/la recepcionista	el/la resepsyo_nees_ta
to recommend	recomendar	rekomen_dar_
refund	el reembolso	el re-em_bolso_
to refuse	negarse	ne_garse_
to relax	relajarse	rela_harse_
to rent	alquilar	alkee_lar_
to request	pedir	pe_deer_
reservation	la reserva	la re_ser_ba
to reserve	reservar	reser_bar_
retired	jubilado/a	hoobee_la_do/a
rich	rico/a	_reeko_/a
to ride	montar a caballo	mon_tar_ a ka_ba_yo
right	la derecha	la de_re_cha
to be right	tener razón	te_ner_ ra_son_
to ring	llamar	ya_mar_
road	la carretera	la karre_te_ra

to rob	robar	_ro_bar

Most Latin American countries have high robbery rates. Watch your pockets and bags.

room	la habitación	la abeeta_syon_
route	la ruta	la _roo_ta
rude	grosero/a	gro_se_ro/a
ruins	las ruinas	las roo_ee_nas
to run	correr	ko_rrer_

S

safe	seguro/a	se_goo_ro/a
Scotland	Escocia	es_ko_sya
Scottish	escocés/esa	es_ko_ses/esa
sea	el mar	el mar
seat	el asiento	al as_yen_to
seat belt	el cinturón de seguridad	el seentoo_ron_ de segooree_dad_
sedative	el sedante	el se_dan_te
see you later	hasta luego	_as_ta _lwe_go
to sell	vender	ben_der_
to send	enviar	en_byar_
sensible	sensato/a	sen_sa_to/a
September	septiembre	set_yem_bre
service	el servicio	el ser_bee_syo
shop	la tienda	la _tyen_da
shopping	las compras	las _kom_pras
shopping centre	el centro comercial	el _sen_tro komer_syal_

short	corto/a	korto/a
to show	mostrar	mostrar
shut	cerrado/a	serrado/a
sign	la señal	la senyal
to sign	firmar	feermar
signature	la firma	la feerma
since	desde	desde
sister	la hermana	la ermana
ski	el esquí	el eskee
to sleep	dormir	dormeer
slow	despacio	despasyo
small	pequeño/a	pekenyo/a
to smoke	fumar	foomar
soft	suave	sooabe
some	algunos/as	algoonos/as
something	algo	algo
son	el hijo	el eeho
soon	pronto	pronto
south	el sur	el soor
South Africa	Sudáfrica	soodaphreeka
South African	sudafricano/a	soodaphreekano/a
Spain	España	espanya
Spanish	español/a	espanyol/a
speed	la velocidad	la beloseedad
to spell	deletrear	deletrear
sport	el deporte	el deporte
staff	el personal	personal
stamp	el sello	el seyo
to start	empezar	empesar
to start (car)	poner en marcha	poner en marcha
station	la estación	la estasyon
sterling pound	la libra esterlina	la leebra esterleena
to stop	parar	parar
straight	recto/a	rekto/a
street	la calle	la kaye
stress	el estrés	el estres

suitcase	la maleta	la maletta

If luggage goes astray, ask "¿Donde está mi maleta?" (where is my bag?).

sun	el sol	el sol
sunglasses	las gafas de sol	las gaphas de sol
surname	el apellido	el apeyeedo
swimming pool	la piscina	la peeseena
symptom	el síntoma	el seentoma

T

table	la mesa	la mesa
to take	tomar	tomar
tall	alto/a	alto/a
tampons	los tampones	los tampones
tax	el impuesto	el eempooesto

taxi	el taxi	el taksee
taxi rank	la parada de taxis	la parada de taksees
telephone	el teléfono	el telephono
television	la televisión	la telebeesyon
terrace	la terraza	la terrasa
to text	mandar un mensaje al celular	mandar un mensahe al seloolar
that	ese/a	ese/a
theft	el robo	el robo
then	entonces	entonses
there	allí	ayee
thing	la cosa	la kosa
to think	pensar	pensar

| thirsty | sediento/a | sedyento/a |

"I am thirsty" is "**tengo sed**" (literally "I have thirst").

this	este/a	este/a
through	a través	a trabes
ticket (bus)	el boleto	el boleto
ticket (cinema)	la entrada	la entrada
ticket (parking)	la multa	la moolta
ticket (shopping)	el recibo	el reseebo
ticket office	la taquilla	la takeeya
time	el tiempo	el tyempo
time (clock)	la hora	la ora
timetable	el horario	el oraryo
tip (money)	la propina	la propeena
tired	cansado/a	kansado/a
to	a	a
today	hoy	oy
toilet	los sanitarios	los saneetaryos
tomorrow	mañana	manyana
tonight	esta noche	esta noche
too	también	tambyen
tourist office	la oficina de turismo	la opheeseena de tooreesmo
town	la ciudad	la theeoodad
train	el tren	el tren
tram	el tranvía	el trambeea
to translate	traducir	tradooseer
travel	el viaje	el beeahe
true	verdadero/a	berdadero/a
typical	típico/a	teepeeko/a

U

ugly	feo/a	feo/a
ulcer	la úlcera	la oolsera
umbrella	el paraguas	el paragwas
uncomfortable	incómodo/a	eenkomodo/a
unconcious	inconsciente	eenkonsyente
under	debajo (de)	debaho (de)
underground (tube)	el metro	el metro

to understand	**entender**	*entender*
underwear	**la ropa interior**	*la ropa eenteryor*
unemployed	**desempleado/a**	*desempleado/a*
unpleasant	**desagradable**	*desagradable*
up	**arriba**	*areeba*
urgent	**urgente**	*oorhente*
to use	**usar**	*oosar*
useful	**útil**	*ooteel*
usually	**normalmente**	*normalmente*

V

vaccination	**la vacuna**	*la bakoona*
valid	**válido/a**	*baleedo/a*
value	**el valor**	*el balor*
valuables	**los objetos de valor**	*los obhetos de balor*
VAT	**el IVA**	*el eeba*
vegetarian	**vegetariano/a**	*behetaryano/a*
very	**muy**	*mooy*
visa	**el visado**	*el beesado*
visit	**la visita**	*la beeseeta*
to visit	**visitar**	*beeseetar*
to vomit	**vomitar**	*bomeetar*

W

waiter/waitress	**el/la camarero/a/el/ la mozo/a**	*el/la camarero/el/ la moso/a*
waiting room	**la sala de espera**	*la sala de espera*
Wales	**Gales**	*gales*
to walk	**caminar**	*kameenar*
wallet	**la cartera**	*la kartera*
to want	**querer**	*kerer*
to wash	**lavar**	*labar*
watch	**el reloj**	*el reloh*
to watch	**mirar**	*meerar*
water	**agua**	*agwa*
water sports	**los deportes acuáticos**	*los deportes agwateekos*
way (manner)	**la manera**	*la manera*
way (route)	**el camino**	*el kameeno*
way in	**la entrada**	*la entrada*
way out	**la salida**	*la saleeda*

| **weather** | **el tiempo** | *el tyempo* |

Rain often falls in short, intense bursts in tropical climes. The squall could pass, as you shelter under a **palapa** (thatched hut).

web	**la internet**	*la eenternet*
website	**la página web**	*la paheena web*
week	**la semana**	*la semana*
weekday	**el día laborable**	*el deea laborable*
weekend	**el fin de semana**	*el feen de semana*
welcome	**bienvenido/a**	*byenbeneedo/a*
well	**bien**	*byen*

English	Spanish	Pronunciation
Welsh	galés/esa	_gales/esa_
west	el oeste	_el oeste_
what?	¿qué?	_keh?_
wheelchair	la silla de ruedas	_sa seeya de rooedas_
when?	¿cuándo?	_kwando?_
where?	¿dónde?	_dondeh?_
which?	¿cuál?	_kwal?_
while	mientras	_myentras_
who?	¿quién?	_kyen?_
why?	¿por qué?	_por keh?_
wife	la esposa	_la esposa_
to win	ganar	_ganar_
with	con	_kon_
without	sin	_seen_
woman	la mujer	_la mooher_
wonderful	maravilloso/a	_marabeeyoso/a_
word	la palabra	_la palabra_
work	el trabajo	_el trabaho_
to work (machine)	funcionar	_foonsyonar_
to work (person)	trabajar	_trabahar_
world	el mundo	_el moondo_
worried	preocupado/a	_preokoopado/a_
worse	peor	_peor_
to write	escribir	_eskreebeer_
wrong (mistaken)	equivocado/a	_ekeebokado/a_

X

x-ray	la radiografía	_la radyographeea_
to x-ray	hacer una radiografía	_aser oona radyographeea_
x-rays	los rayos x	_los rayos ekees_

Y

yacht	el yate	_el yate_
year	el año	_el anyo_
yearly	anual	_anooal_
yellow pages	las páginas amarillas	_las paheenas amareeyas_
yes	sí	_see_
yesterday	ayer	_ayer_
yet	todavía	_todabeea_
you (formal)	usted	_oosted_
you (informal)	tú	_too_
young	joven	_hoben_
your (formal)	su/s	_soo/s_
your (informal)	tu/s	_too/s_
youth hostel	el albergue juvenil	_el alberge hoobeneel_

Z

zebra crossing	el paso de cebra	_el paso de sebra_
zero	el cero	_el sero_
zip	la cremallera	_la kremayera_
zone	la zona	_la sona_
zoo	el zoo	_el so_

Latin American Spanish-English dictionary

A

a	*a*	to
a través	*a trabes*	through
abajo	*abaho*	down
abierto/a	*abyerto/a*	open
abogado/a, el/la	*el/la abogado/a*	lawyer
abril	*abreel*	April
abrir	*abreer*	to open
accidente, el	*el akseedente*	accident
aduana, la	*la adooana*	customs
aeropuerto, el	*el aeropooerto*	airport
agencia de viajes, la	*la ahensya de beeahes*	travel agency
agosto	*agosto*	August

---

agua *agwa* **water**
Watch the water: ask for **agua purificada** (purified)
in bottles and avoid ice cubes.

---

ahora	*aora*	now
al lado de	*al lado de*	next to
al menos	*al menos*	at least
alarma, la	*la alarma*	alarm
albergue juvenil, el	*el alberge hoobeneel*	youth hostel
alergia, la	*la alerhya*	allergy
algo	*algo*	something
alguno/a(s)	*algoono/a(s)*	any, some
allí	*ayee*	there
alojamiento, el	*el alohamyento*	accommodation
alquilar	*alkeelar*	to rent
alquiler, el	*el alkeeler*	rent
alrededor	*alrededor*	around
alto/a	*alto/a*	tall
amable	*amable*	kind (nice)
ambulancia, la	*la amboolansya*	ambulance
América	*amereeka*	America
americano/a	*amereekano/a*	American
amigo/a, el/la	*el/la ameego/a*	friend
amueblado/a	*amooeblado/a*	furnished
andén, el	*el anden*	platform
aniversario, el	*el aneebersaryo*	anniversary
antes (de)	*antes (de)*	before
anual	*anooal*	yearly
año, el	*el anyo*	year
apagado/a	*apagado/a*	switched off
aparcar	*aparkar*	to park
apartamento, el	*el apartamento*	apartment
apellido, el	*el apeyeedo*	surname

aquí	*akee*	here
área, el	*el area*	area
arriba	*areeba*	up

| **arte, el** | ***el arte*** | **art** |

Oaxaca, Mexico City and Monterrey are considered the centres of Mexican contemporary art.

asiento, el	*el asyento*	seat
aspirina, la	*la aspeereena*	aspirin
atacar	*atakar*	to attack
atrás	*atras*	back (place)
Australia	*awstralya*	Australia
australiano/a	*awstralyano/a*	Australian
autobús, el	*el awtoboos*	bus
autoservicio, el	*el awtoserbeesyo*	self-service
avión, el	*el abyon*	aeroplane
ayer	*ayer*	yesterday
ayudar	*ayoodar*	to help
ayuntamiento, el	*el ayoontamyento*	town hall

B

bahía, la	*la baeea*	bay (coast)
baño, el	*el banyo*	bath
bar, el	*el bar*	bar (pub)
barato/a	*barato/a*	cheap
barbacoa, la	*barbakoa*	barbecue
barrio, el	*el baryo*	neighbourhood
bastante	*bastante*	enough
bebé, el	*el bebeh*	baby

| **beber** | ***beber*** | **drink** |

A lesson in drinking Tequila: knock back the shot, lick salt from your hand and suck a segment of lime.

besar	*besar*	to kiss
beso, el	*el beso*	kiss
biblioteca, la	*la beeblyoteka*	library
bicicleta, la	*la beeseekletta*	bicycle
bien	*byen*	well
bienvenido/a	*byenbeneedo/a*	welcome
billete, el (bus)	*el beeyete*	ticket
billete, el (money)	*el beeyete*	note
bodega, la	*la bodega*	wine cellar, restaurant
bolsa, la	*la bolsa*	bag
bonito/a (people)	*boneeto/a*	pretty
bonito/a (things)	*boneeto/a*	nice
bosque, el	*el boske*	forest
bote, el	*el bote*	boat
botella, la	*la boteya*	bottle

bronceador, el	el bronseador	suntan lotion
bueno/a	bweno/a	good
bufé, el	el boopheh	buffet
buscar	booskar	to look for
butacas, las	las bootakas	stalls (theatre)
buzón, el	el booson	postbox

C

cafetería, la	la kaphetereea	café
cajero automático, el	el kahero awtomateeko	cash point
calculadora, la	la kalkooladora	calculator
caliente	kalyente	hot
calle, la	la kaye	street
calmante, el	el kalmante	painkiller
calor, el	el kalor	heat
cámara fotográfica, la	la kamara photographeeka	camera
camarero/a, el/la	el/la kamarero/a	waiter/tress
cambiar	kambyar	to change
cambio, el	el kambeeo	exchange rate
caminar	kameenar	to walk
camino, el	el kameeno	way (route)
campo, el	el kampo	countryside
campo de golf, el	el kampo de golph	golf course
cancelar	kanselar	to cancel
cansado/a	kansado/a	tired
cantidad, la	la kanteedad	quantity
carnet de identidad, el	el kameh de eedenteedad	identity card
carretera, la	la karretera	road
carro, el	el karro	car
carta, la	la karta	letter
cartera, la	la kartera	wallet
casa de cambio, la	la kasa de kambyo	bureau de change
casado/a	kasado/a	married
casino, el	el kaseeno	casino
catedral, la	la katedral	cathedral
cd, el	el sedeh	cd
centro, el	el sentro	centre
centro comercial, el	el sentro komersyal	shopping centre
cerca	serka	near
cerrado/a	serrado/a	closed
cerrar	serrar	to close
cheque, el	el cheke	cheque
chico/a, el/la	el/la cheeko/a	boy/girl
ciclismo, el	el seekleesmo	cycling
cigarrillo, el	el seegareeyo	cigarette

cine	seene	cinema

Catch some **cine latinoamericano** to ease yourself into the holiday mood.

cinturón de seguridad, el	el seentooron de segooreedad	seat belt
cita, la	la seeta	appointment

ciudad, la	*la seeoodad*	city, town
clase, la	*la klase*	kind (sort)
cliente, el	*el klyente*	customer
club, el	*el kloob*	club
cobrar	*kobrar*	to charge
cola, la	*la cola*	queue
color, el	*el kolor*	colour
comedor, el	*el komedor*	dining room
comer	*komer*	to eat
¿cómo?	*komo?*	how?
comprar	*komprar*	to buy
compras, las	*las kompras*	shopping
compresa, la	*le kompresa*	sanitary towel
computadora, la	*la kompootadora*	computer
con	*kon*	with
conductor/a, el/la	*el/la kondooktor/a*	driver
confirmación, la	*la konpheermasyon*	confirmation
confirmar	*konpheermar*	to confirm
conocer	*konoser*	to know (person)
concurso, el	*el konkoorso*	quiz
consulado, el	*el konsoolado*	consulate
contagioso/a	*kontahyoso/a*	contagious
correo, el	*el korreo*	mail, post
correo electrónico, el	*el korreo elektroneeko*	e-mail
correr	*korrer*	to run
corrida de toros, la	*la korreeda de torros*	bullfight
cosa, la	*la kosa*	thing
costa, la	*la kosta*	coast
costar	*kostar*	to cost
crema, la	*la krema*	cream
crema de afeitar, la	*la krema de afeytar*	shaving cream

crema para después del sol	*la krema para despwes del sol*	after-sun lotion

Something to slather on after days in scorching Caribbean rays: after-sun lotion.

¿cuál?	*kwal?*	which?
¿cuándo?	*kwando?*	when?
¿cuánto?	*kwanto?*	how much?
¿cuánto tiempo?	*kwanto tyempo?*	how long?
cuarto, el	*el kwarto*	quarter
cuenta, la	*la kwenta*	bill

D

daño/s, el/los	*el/los danyo/s*	damage
dar	*dar*	to give
de/desde	*de/desde*	from
de acuerdo	*de akwerdo*	ok
¡de prisa!	*de preesa!*	hurry up!
de repente	*de repente*	suddenly
debajo (de)	*debaho (de)*	below
deletrear	*deletrear*	to spell

delito, el	el deleeto	crime
dentro (de)	dentro (de)	inside
dependiente/a, el/la	el/la dependyente/a	shop assistant
deporte, el	el deporte	sport
deportes acuáticos, los	los deportes agwateekos	water sports
deprisa	depreesa	quickly
derecha, la	la derecha	right
desagradable	desagradable	unpleasant
desaparecido/a	desapareseedo/a	missing
descuento, el	el deskwento	discount
desde	desde	since
desempleado/a	desempleado/a	unemployed
deshidratar	deseedratar	to dehydrate
desinfectante, el	el deseenphektante	disinfectant
despacio	despasyo	slow
después	despwes	after
detrás (de)	detras (de)	behind
día, el	el deea	day
día laborable, el	el deea laborable	weekday
diciembre	deesyembre	December
difícil	deepheesyl	difficult
dinero, el	el deenero	money
dinero en efectivo, el	el deenero en ephekteebo	cash
director/a, el/la	el/la deerektor/a	manager
discapacitado/a	deeskapaseetado/a	disable
discoteca, la	la deeskoteka	disco
disponible	deesponeeble	available
divertirse	deeberteerse	to enjoy
doble	doble	double
doler	doler	to hurt
¿dónde?	dondeh?	where?
dormir	dormeer	to sleep
drogas, las	las drogas	drugs
ducha, la	la doocha	shower
dueño/a, el/la	el/la dwenyo/a	owner
durante	doorante	during

E

echar de menos	echar de menos	to miss (a person)
elevador, el	el elebador	lift
embajada, la	la embahada	embassy
emergencia, la	la emerhensya	emergency
empezar	empesar	to start
en	en	in, on, at
en avión	en abyon	by plane
en casa	en kasa	at home
en ningún sitio	en neengoon seeteeo	nowhere
encontrar	enkontrar	to meet
enero	enero	January
enfermo/a	enfermo/a	ill
enfrente (de)	enphrente (de)	opposite (place)
entender	entender	to understand
entonces	entonses	then

entrada, la	*la entrada*	ticket (cinema)
entrada, la	*la entrada*	way in

entre	***entre***	**between**

Positioned between two oceans, Costa Rica has a long coastline and an abundance of beautiful beaches.

enviar	*enbyar*	to send
equipaje, el	*el ekeepahe*	luggage
equivocado/a	*ekeebokado/a*	mistaken
error, el	*el error*	error
escaleras, las	*las eskaleras*	stairs
escasez, la	*la eskases*	shortage
escocés/esa	*eskoses/esa*	Scottish
Escocia	*eskosya*	Scotland
escribir	*eskreebeer*	to write
escuchar	*eskoochar*	to listen to
ese/a	*ese/a*	that
España	*espanya*	Spain
español/a	*espanyol/a*	Spanish
espectáculo, el	*el espektakoolo*	show
esposa, la	*la esposa*	wife
esquí, el	*el eskee*	ski
estación, la	*la estasyon*	station
estación de autobuses, la	*la estasyon de awtobooses*	bus station
estacionamiento, el	*el estasyonamyento*	parking
estadio, el	*el estadyo*	stadium
este/a	*este/a*	this
estrés, el	*el estres*	stress
estropeado/a	*estropeado/a*	out of order
etiqueta, la	*la eteeketta*	label
exactamente	*eksaktamente*	exactly
exportar	*eksportar*	to export
exposición, la	*la eksposeesyon*	exhibition

F

facturar	*phaktoorar*	to check in (airport)
favorito/a	*faboreeto/a*	favourite
febrero	*febrero*	February
fecha, la	*la phecha*	date (calendar)
¡felicidades!	*feleeseedades!*	congratulations!
feo/a	*feo/a*	ugly

ferrocarril, el	***el pherrokarryl***	**railway**

Peru's railway makes the Andes and the Inca trail accessible to locals and visitors. For a ride to rival all others, take the famously spectacular route from Cuzco to Machu Pichu.

fiesta, la	*la fyesta*	holiday, party

fin de semana, el	*el feen de semana*	weekend
firma, la	*la feerma*	signature
firmar	*feermar*	to sign
foto, la	*la photo*	photo
fresco/a	*phresko/a*	cool
frío/a	*phreeo/a*	cold
fuego, el	*el phwego*	fire
fuera (de)	*phwera (de)*	outside
fumar	*foomar*	to smoke
funcionar	*foonsyonar*	to work (machine)
fútbol	*phootbol*	football

G

gafas de sol, las	*las gaphas de sol*	sunglasses
galería, la	*la galereea*	gallery
Gales	*hales*	Wales
galés/esa	*hales/esa*	Welsh
ganar	*ganar*	to win
garage, el	*el garahe*	garage
garantía, la	*la garanteea*	guarantee
gas, el	*el gas*	gas
gasolinera, la	*la gasoleenera*	filling station
gente, la	*la hente*	people
golf, el	*el golph*	golf
golpear	*golpear*	to knock
gorro de baño, el	*el gorro de banyo*	bathing cap
grande	*grande*	big
gratis	*gratees*	free (money)
gripe, la	*la greepe*	flu
grosero/a	*grosero/a*	rude
grupo, el	*el groopo*	group
guardar	*gwardar*	to keep
guía, la	*la geea*	guide
guía de conversación, la	*la geea de konbersasyon*	phrase book
gustar	*goostar*	to like

H

habitación, la	*la abeetasyon*	room
hace	*ase*	ago
hacer	*aser*	to make
hacer una radiografía	*aser oona radyographeea*	to x-ray
hermano/a, el/la	*el/la ermano/a*	brother/sister
hijo/a, el/la	*el/la eeho/a*	son/daughter
hoja de afeitar, la	*la oha de afeytar*	razor blade

hombre	*ombre*	**man**

'Yo soy un hombre sincero...' (I am a sincere man...), the first line of Cuba's famous song Guantanamera.

homosexual	*omoseksooal*	homosexual
hora, la	*la ora*	time (clock)

horario, el	*el oraryo*	timetable
hospital, el	*el ospeetal*	hospital
hoy	*oy*	today

I

idioma, el	*el eedeeoma*	language
iglesia, la	*la eeglesya*	church
importante	*eemportante*	important
importar	*eemportar*	to import
impreso, el	*el eempreso*	form (document)
impuesto, el	*el eempooesto*	tax
impuestos, los	*los eempooestos*	duty (tax)
incómodo/a	*eenkomodo/a*	uncomfortable
inconsciente	*eenkonsyente*	unconcious
información, la	*la eenphormasyon*	information
Inglaterra	*eenglaterra*	England
inglés/esa	*eengles/esa*	English
inmediatamente	*eemedyatamente*	immediately
instalaciones, las	*las eenstalasyones*	facilities
instrucciones, las	*las eenstrooksyones*	directions
interesante	*eenteresante*	interesting
internacional	*eenternasyonal*	international
internet, la	*la eenternet*	web
intoxicación alimenticia, la	*la eentokseekasyon aleementeesya*	food poisoning
ir	*eer*	to go
Irlanda	*eerlanda*	Ireland
irlandés/esa	*eerlandes/esa*	Irish
isla, la	*la eesla*	island
itinerario, el	*el eeteeneraryo*	itinerary
IVA, el	*el eeba*	VAT
izquierda, la	*la eeskyerda*	left

J

joven	*hoben*	young
jubilado/a	*hoobeelado/a*	retired
julio	*hoolyo*	July
junio	*hoonyo*	June

K

kilo, el	*el keelo*	kilo
kilometraje, el	*el keelometrahe*	mileage
kiosko, el	*el keeosko*	newstand

L

lavandería, la	*la labandereea*	launderette
lavar	*labar*	to wash
lavar en seco	*labar en sekko*	to dry clean
lejos	*lehos*	far
lentes, las	*las lentes*	glasses
lentillas, las	*las lenteeyas*	contact lenses
libra esterlina, la	*la leebra esterleena*	sterling pound
libre	*leebre*	free, vacant
libre de impuestos	*leebre de eempooestos*	tax free
libro, el	*el leebro*	book

licencia de manejar	la leesensya de manehar	driving licence
listo/a	leesto/a	ready
llamar	yamar	to call
llamar por teléfono	yamar por telephono	to phone
llave, la	la yabe	key
llavero, el	el yabero	key ring
llegada, la	la yegada	arrival
lluvia, la	la yoobya	rain
local	lokal	local

lugar	*loogar*	**place**

Looking for a good place to dance salsa? Then ask:
¿Un buen lugar para bailar?

M

madre, la	la madre	mother
maleta, la	la maletta	suitcase
malo/a	malo/a	off (food)
mancha, la	la mancha	stain
mandar por fax	mandar por phaks	to fax
mandar un mensaje al celular	mandar un mensahe al seloolar	to text
manejar	manehar	to drive
manera, la	la manera	manner
mañana	manyana	tomorrow
mapa, el	el mapa	map (road)
mar, el	el mar	sea
maravilloso/a	marabeeyoso/a	wonderful
marcar	markar	to dial
marido, el	el mareedo	husband
marzo	marso	March
más	mas	more
matar	matar	to kill
mayo	mayo	May
mayoría, la	la mayoreea	most
mecánico/a, el/la	el/la mekaneeko/a	mechanic
medianoche, la	la medyanoche	midnight
medicina, la	la medeeseena	drug
médico/a, el/la	el/la medeeko/a	doctor
medio/a	medyo/a	half
mediodía, el	el medyodeea	midday
medusa, la	la medoosa	jellyfish
mejor	mehor	better
mejor, el/la/lo	el/la/lo mehor	the best
menos	menos	less
mercado, el	el merkado	market
mesa, la	la mesa	table
metro, el	el metro	underground (tube)
mi	mee	my
mientras	myentras	while
mínimo/a	meeneemo/a	minimum
minuto, el	el meenooto	minute
mirar	meerar	to look

molestar	molestar	to disturb
momento, el	el momento	moment
moneda, la	la moneda	currency
montar a caballo	montar a kabayo	to ride a horse
mosquito, el	el moskeeto	mosquito
mostrar	mostrar	to show
moto acuática, la	la moto akwateeka	jet ski
mucho	moocho	much
muchos/as	moochos/as	many
mujer, la	la mooher	woman
multa, la	la moolta	ticket (parking)

| **mundo** | **moondo** | **world** |

The **Mundo Latino** has a strong music culture, with ever more latino singers enjoying international success.

museo, el	el mooseo	museum
musical, el	el mooseekal	musical
muy	mooy	very

N

nacionalidad, la	la nasyonalidad	nationality
nada	nada	nothing
necesario/a	nesesaryo/a	necessary
necesitar	neseseetar	to need
negarse	negarse	to refuse
negocio, el	el negosyo	business
niño/a, el/la	el/la neenyo/a	child
noche, la	la noche	night
nombre, el	el nombre	name
normalmente	normalmente	usually
norte, el	el norte	north
noticias, las	las noteesyas	news
noviembre	nobyembre	November
nuevo/a	nwebo/a	new
número, el	el noomero	number
nunca	noonka	never

O

o	o	or
objeto, el	el obheto	object
objetos de valor, los	los obhetos de balor	valuables
objetos perdidos, los	los obhetos perdeedos	lost property
obtener	obtener	to get
octubre	oktoobre	October
oeste, el	el oeste	west
oficina, la	la opheeseena	office
oficina de correos, la	la opheeseena de korreos	post office
oficina de turismo, la	la opheeseena de tooreesmo	tourist office
óptica, la	la opteeka	optician's
organizar	organeesar	to arrange

otra vez	_otra bes_	again

Come to the Caribbean once and you're bound to come **otra vez.**

otro/a	_otro/a_	other
otro/a(s)	_otro/a(s)_	another
oxígeno, el	el _okseeheno_	oxygen

P

padre, el	el _padre_	father
padres, los	los _padres_	parents
pagar	_pagar_	to pay
página web, la	la _paheena_ web	website
páginas amarillas, las	las _paheenas amareeyas_	yellow pages
país, el	el _pays_	country
palabra, la	la _palabra_	word
papel de escribir, el	el _papel_ de _eskreebeer_	writing paper
papel de fumar, el	el _papel_ de _fumar_	cigarette paper
papelería, la	la _papelereea_	stationer's
par, el	el _par_	pair
para	_para_	for
parada de autobús, la	la _parada_ de _awtoboos_	bus stop
parada de taxis, la	la _parada_ de _taksees_	taxi rank
paraguas, el	el _paragwas_	umbrella
parar	_parar_	to stop
parque, el	el _parke_	park
pasaporte, el	el _pasaporte_	passport
paso de cebra, el	el _paso_ de _sebra_	zebra crossing
peaje, el	el _peahe_	toll
pedir	_pedeer_	to order
película, la	la _peleecoola_	film (cinema)
peligro, el	el _peleegro_	danger
pelo, el	el _pelo_	hair
peluquería, la	la _pelookereea_	hairdresser's
pensar	_pensar_	to think
peor	_peor_	worse
pequeño/a	_pekenyo/a_	small
perder	_perder_	to lose
perder	_perder_	to miss (a train)
periódico, el	el _peryodeeko_	newspaper
pero	_pero_	but
persona, la	la _persona_	person
personal	_personal_	staff

picadura de mosquito	_peekadoora de moskeeto_	mosquito bite

Beware harmful mosquito bites – vaccinations before you leave are a sensible precaution.

piscina, la	la peeseena	swimming pool
pista de tenis, la	la peesta de tenees	tennis court
plano, el	el plano	map (city)
playa, la	la playa	beach
playa nudista, la	la playa noodeesta	nudist beach
poco, un	oon poko	a bit
poder	poder	to be able
policía, la	la poleeseea	police
poner	poner	to put
poner en marcha	poner en marcha	to start (car)
ponerse en contacto	ponerse en kontakto	to contact
por (place)	por	by (via)
por (time)	por	for
por fin	por pheen	at last
por la noche	por la noche	overnight
¿por qué?	por keh?	why?
porque	porkeh	because
posible	poseeble	possible
precio, el	el presyo	charge
preferir	prefeereer	to prefer
prefijo, el	el prepheeho	area code
pregunta, la	la pregoonta	question
preguntar	pregoontar	to ask
preocupado/a	preokoopado/a	worried
primeros auxilios, los	los preemeros awkseelyos	first aid
principal	preenseepal	main
privado/a	preebado/a	private
probablemente	probablemente	probably
probador, el	el probador	fitting room
problema, el	el problema	problem
pronto	pronto	soon
propina, la	la propeena	tip (money)
pub, el	el poob	pub
puerto, el	el pwerto	port (sea)
puro, el	el pooro	cigar

Q

¿qué?	keh?	what?
quemar	kemar	to burn
querer	kerer	to want
¿quién?	kyen?	who?
quiosco, el	el kyosko	kiosk

| quizás | keesas | perhaps |

'Perhaps, perhaps, perhaps'. Nat King Cole made this song famous worldwide.

R

radio, la	la radyo	radio
radiografía, la	la radyographeea	x-ray
rápido/a	rapeedo/a	fast

rápido/a	*rapeedo/a*	express (train)
rayos x, los	*los rayos ekees*	x-rays
real	*real*	real
recado, el	*el rekado*	message
recepción, la	*la rethepsyon*	reception
recepcionista, el/la	*el/la rethepsyoneesta*	receptionist
receta, la	*la reseta*	prescription
recibir	*reseebeer*	to receive
recibo, el	*el reseebo*	receipt
reclamación, la	*la reklamasyon*	complaint
reclamar	*reklamar*	to complain
recomendar	*rekomendar*	to recommend
recto/a	*rekto/a*	straight
reembolso, el	*el re-embolso*	refund
registrarse	*reheestrarse*	to check in (hotel)
relajarse	*relaharse*	to relax
reloj, el	*el reloh*	watch
reserva, la	*la reserba*	reservation
reservar	*reserbar*	to reserve
responder	*responder*	to answer
retrasado/a	*retrasado/a*	delayed
retraso, el	*el retraso*	delay
reunión, la	*la reoonyon*	meeting
rico/a	*reeko/a*	rich

rico/a	*reeko/a*	tasty

When referring to food: delicious. If you're really enjoying your meal, express yourself: **¡Muy rico!**

robar	*robar*	to rob
robo, el	*el robo*	theft
rollo, el	*el royo*	film (camera)
ropa, la	*la ropa*	clothes
ropa interior, la	*la ropa eenteryor*	underwear
ruinas, las	*las rooeenas*	ruins
ruta, la	*la roota*	route

S

saber	*saber*	to know (knowledge)
sala de espera, la	*la sala de espera*	waiting room
sala de fiestas, la	*la sala de fyestas*	nightclub
salida, la	*la saleeda*	way out
salida de incendios, la	*la saleeda de eensendyos*	fire exit
salir	*saleer*	to leave
sanitarios, los	*los saneetaryos*	toilet
sanitarios de caballeros, los	*los saneetaryos de kabayeros*	gents toilets
sanitarios de señoras, los	*los saneetaryos de senyoras*	ladies toilets
sauna, la	*la saona*	sauna
sedante, el	*el sedante*	sedative
sediento/a	*sedyento/a*	thirsty

seguro, el	*el segooro*	insurance
seguro/a	*segooro/a*	safe
sello, el	*el seyo*	stamp
semana, la	*la semana*	week
sensato/a	*sensato/a*	sensible
señal, la	*la senyal*	sign
señor/ora, el/la	*el/la senyor/ora*	sir/lady
septiembre	*setyembre*	September

ser/estar	*ser/estar*	to be

Two Spanish verbs for the English "to be" – confusing!
Here's a good tip: **ser** is for permanent things (**soy latino**:
I'm Latin), **estar** for temporary (**estoy cansado**: I'm tired)

servicio, el	*el serbeesyo*	service
servir	*serbeer*	to serve
sí	*see*	yes
SIDA, el	*el seeda*	AIDS
siguiente, el/la	*el/la seegyente*	next
silla de ruedas, la	*la seeya de rooedas*	wheelchair
simpático/a	*seempateeko/a*	nice (people)
sin	*seen*	without
síntoma, el	*el seentoma*	symptom
sobre	*sobre*	concerning
socorrista, el/la	*el/la sokorreesta*	lifeguard
¡socorro!	*sokorro!*	help!
sol, el	*el sol*	sun
sólo	*solo*	only
somnífero, el	*el somneephero*	sleeping pill
su/s	*soo/s*	your (formal)
suave	*sooabe*	soft
sucio/a	*soosyo/a*	dirty
Sudáfrica	*soodaphreeka*	South Africa
sudafricano/a	*soodaphreekano/a*	South African
sur, el	*el soor*	south

T

tabaco, el	*el tabako*	tobacco
también	*tambyen*	too
tampones, los	*los tampones*	tampons
taquilla, la	*la takeeya*	box office
tarde	*tarde*	late

tarjeta de crédito, la	*la tarhetta de kredeeto*	credit card

Plástico is not as popular here as it is in the UK. Make
sure you carry enough cash with you, as not all shops
will accept credit cards.

tarjeta de embarque, la	*la tarhetta de embarkeh*	boarding card

taxi, el	el *taksee*	taxi
teclado, el	el te*kla*do	keyboard
telefonista, el/la	el/la telepho*nees*ta	operator
teléfono, el	el te*lepho*no	phone
teléfono celular, el	el te*lepho*no seloo*lar*	mobile phone
televisión, la	la telebee*syon*	television
temprano	tem*pra*no	early
tener	te*ner*	to have
tener hambre	te*ner ambre*	to be hungry
tener que	te*ner* ke	must
tener razón	te*ner* ra*son*	to be right
tenis, el	el te*nees*	tennis
terminar	termee*nar*	to finish
terraza, la	la te*rra*sa	terrace
tiempo, el	el *tyem*po	time, weather
tienda, la	la *tyen*da	shop
tintorería, la	la teentore*reea*	dry cleaner's
típico/a	tee*peeko*/a	typical
todavía	toda*beea*	yet
todo/a(s)	*todo*/a(s)	all
tomar	to*mar*	to take
trabajar	traba*har*	to work (person)
trabajo, el	el tra*ba*ho	work
traducir	tradoo*seer*	to translate
tranquilo/a	tran*keelo*/a	quiet

transporte público	**el trans*por*te *poob*leeko**	**public transport**

Never rely on public transport in Cuba… you'll wait the whole day for the next **guagua** (bus).

tranvía, el	el tram*beea*	tram
tren, el	el tren	train
triste	*trees*te	sad
tú	too	you (informal)
tu/s	too/s	your (informal)

U

úlcera, la	la *ool*sera	ulcer
último/a, el/la	el/la *oolteemo*	last
un/a	oon/a	a(n)
una vez	*oo*na bes	once
urgencias	oor*henseeas*	A&E
urgente	oor*hente*	urgent
urgente	oor*hente*	express (mail)
usar	oo*sar*	to use

usted	**oos*ted***	**you (formal)**

This is the polite form of **tú** (you), widely used in Latin America. Always say **usted** rather than **tú**: you'll make a much better impression!

| útil | _ooteel_ | useful |

V

vacaciones, las	_las bakasyones_	holidays
vacuna, la	_la bakoona_	vaccine
válido/a	_baleedo/a_	valid
valor, el	_el balor_	value

| **vegetariano** | _behetaryano/a_ | **vegetarian** |

Vegetarians do not abound in Latin America and often a so-called **sándwich vegetariano** may actually have ham in it alongside lettuce and tomatoes!

vehículo, el	_el beheekoolo_	vehicle
velocidad, la	_la belotheedad_	sailing boat
velero, el	_el belero_	sailing boat
vender	_bender_	to sell
venir	_beneer_	to come
verdadero/a	_berdadero/a_	true
viaje, el	_el byahe_	journey
violación, la	_la beeolasyon_	rape
visado, el	_el beesado_	visa
visita, la	_la beeseeta_	visit
visitar	_beeseetar_	to visit

| **vitamina** | _beetameena_ | **vitamin** |

Fresh fruit is available everywhere, making it easy to cover your daily vitamin needs.

| vomitar | _bomeetar_ | to vomit |
| vuelo, el | _el booelo_ | flight |

W

| windsurf | _weensoorph_ | windsurfing |

X

| xenofobia, la | _la ksenophobeea_ | xenophobia |
| xenófobo/a | _ksenophobo/a_ | xenophobe |

Y

y	_ee_	and
yate, el	_el yate_	yacht
yogur, el	_el yogoor_	yoghurt

Z

| zona, la | _la sona_ | zone |
| zoo, el | _el so_ | zoo |

Quick reference

Numbers

0	**cero**	*sero*
1	**uno**	*oono*
2	**dos**	*dos*
3	**tres**	*tres*
4	**cuatro**	*kwatro*
5	**cinco**	*seenko*
6	**seis**	*seys*
7	**siete**	*syete*
8	**ocho**	*ocho*
9	**nueve**	*nooebe*
10	**diez**	*dyes*
11	**once**	*onse*
12	**doce**	*dose*
13	**trece**	*trese*
14	**catorce**	*katorse*
15	**quince**	*keense*
16	**dieciséis**	*dyeseeseys*
17	**diecisiete**	*dyeseesyete*
18	**dieciocho**	*dyeseeocho*
19	**diecinueve**	*dyeseenooebe*
20	**veinte**	*bente*
21	**veintiuno**	*benteeuno*
30	**treinta**	*trenta*
40	**cuarenta**	*kwarenta*
50	**cincuenta**	*seenkwenta*
60	**sesenta**	*sesenta*
70	**setenta**	*setenta*
80	**ochenta**	*ochenta*
90	**noventa**	*nobenta*
100	**cien**	*syen*
1000	**mil**	*meel*
1st	**El/la primero/a**	*el/la preemero/a*
2nd	**El/la segundo/a**	*el/la segoondo/a*
3rd	**El/la tercero/a**	*el/la tersero/a*
4th	**El/la cuarto/a**	*el/la kwarto/a*
5th	**El/la quinto/a**	*el/la keento/a*

Weights & Measures

gram (=0.03oz)	**El gramo**	*el gramo*
kilogram (=2.2lb)	**El kilogramo**	*el keelogramo*
centimetre (=0.4in)	**El centímetro**	*el senteemetro*
metre (=1.1yd)	**El metro**	*el metro*
kilometre (=0.6m)	**El kilómetro**	*el keelometro*
litre (=2.1pt)	**El litro**	*el leetro*

Days & time

Monday	**El lunes**	*el loones*
Tuesday	**El martes**	*el martes*
Wednesday	**El miércoles**	*el myerkoles*
Thursday	**El jueves**	*el hooebes*
Friday	**El viernes**	*el byernes*
Saturday	**El sábado**	*el sabado*
Sunday	**El domingo**	*el domeengo*
What time is it?	**¿Qué hora es?**	*keh orah es?*
(Four) o'clock	**Son (las cuatro) en punto**	*son (las kwatro) en poonto*
Quarter past (six)	**Son (las seis) y cuarto**	*son (las seys) ee kwarto*
Half past (eight)	**Son (las ocho) y media**	*son (las ocho) ee medya*
Quarter to (ten)	**Son (las diez) menos cuarto**	*son (las dyes) menos kwarto*
morning	**La mañana**	*la manyana*
afternoon	**La tarde**	*la tarde*
evening	**La tarde**	*la tarde*
night	**La noche**	*la noche*

Months

January	**Enero**	*enero*
February	**Febrero**	*febrero*
March	**Marzo**	*marso*
April	**Abril**	*abreel*
May	**Mayo**	*mayo*
June	**Junio**	*hoonyo*
July	**Julio**	*hoolyo*
August	**Agosto**	*agosto*
September	**Septiembre**	*setyembre*
October	**Octubre**	*octoobre*
November	**Noviembre**	*nobyembre*
December	**Diciembre**	*deesyembre*